Using the Standards
Algebra

Grade 4

by

Melissa Warner Hale

Published by Instructional Fair
an imprint of
Frank Schaffer Publications®

Instructional Fair

Author: Melissa Warner Hale
Editor: Karen Thompson

Frank Schaffer Publications®

Instructional Fair is an imprint of Frank Schaffer Publications.

Send all inquiries to:
Frank Schaffer Publications
8720 Orion Place
Columbus, OH 43240-2111

Using the Standards: Algebra—grade 4

ISBN: 0-7424-2884-2

5 6 7 8 9 10 MAZ 09 08 07 06

Table of Contents

Introduction 4–5
NCTM Algebra Standards
  Correlation Chart. 6
Pretest 7–8

Patterns and Functions
Doing the Bunny Hop 9
Polygon Patterns 10
Shape Patterns 11
Number Parade 12
Percussion Patterns 13
Pattern Match-Up 14
Delightful Designs 15
To Grow or Not to Grow. 16
Going Up or
  Coming Down? 17
The Case of the
  Missing Numbers 18
Rule of Thumb 19
Fill in the Blanks 20
Keeping It Steady 21–22
A Tidy Sum 23
Function Machine. 24
Follow the Rules 25
In and Out. 26
Function Junction 27
In a Word 28–29
Snow Day 30–31
Create Your Own Problems . . . 32
Check Your Skills 33

Situations and Structures
Marble Mayhem 34
Pinching Pennies. 35
Groovy Groupings 36
Principled Products 37
Which Property? 38
Puzzling Properties 39
Making Models 40–41

Model This. 42
Break Down. 43
In the Proper Order 44
Digit Dilemma 45
Number Clues 46
Mystery Numbers. 47
Missing Numbers 48
Solve It! 49
Valuable Variables 50
Solution Pairs 51
A Sporting Chance 52
A Baker's Dozen. 53
Nature Walk 54
Symbol Sense. 55
Alphabet Soup 56
Triple Tease 57
Exceptional Equations 58–59
That's a Puzzler 60
Picture Perfect. 61
A Sweet Treat. 62
Taking a Trip 63
Finding Unknowns. 64–65
Perplexing Problems 66–67
How Far? 68
How Fast? 69
How Long? 70
Create Your Own Problems . . . 71
Check Your Skills. 72–73

Models
Weighty Matters. 74–75
Container Calculations. . . . 76–77
Recreational Rectangles . . . 78–79
Perimeter Puzzle 80–81
To the Max. 82–83
Create Your Own Problems . . . 84
Check Your Skills 85

Changes in Context
Stretched to the Limit 86–87
Up and Down. 88–89
FAN-tastic! 90–91
Making Money 92–93
Ferris Wheel. 94–95
Cube Curiosity 96–97
Building Pyramids 98–99
Dollars and Sense. 100–101
Speeding Spectacular 102
Go Gravity! 103
Give It Some Bounce. . . 104–105
Create Your Own Problems . . 106
Check Your Skills 107–108

Posttest 109–110
Answer Key 111–120
Vocabulary Cards 121–128

0-7424-2884-2 *Using the Standards—Algebra*

Introduction

NCTM Standards: This book focuses on the National Council of Teachers of Mathematics (NCTM) content standards for Algebra. The activities are divided into four main sections based on the NCTM Algebra standards. NCTM defines the standards as follows:

Patterns and Functions: Students will learn to understand patterns, relations, and functions. For grades 3–5, this includes describing, extending, and making generalizations about geometric and numeric patterns as well as representing and analyzing patterns and functions using words, tables, and graphs.

Situations and Structures: Students will be able to represent and analyze mathematical situations and structures using algebraic symbols. The specific skills used in grades 3–5 are identifying mathematical properties and using them to compute with whole numbers, representing an unknown quantity with a letter or symbol, and expressing mathematical relationships using equations.

Models: Students will use mathematical models to represent and understand numerical relationships. In grades 3–5 this includes using objects and representations such as graphs, tables, and equations.

Changes in Context: Students will learn to analyze change in various contexts. For grades 3–5, this includes investigating how change in one variable relates to a change in a second variable. Students will also identify, describe, and compare situations with constant or varying rates of change.

Each activity in the book also incorporates at least one of the five NCTM process standards:

 Problem Solving

 Communication

 Reasoning and Proof

 Connections

 Representation

Each activity is referenced in the **NCTM Algebra Standards Correlation Chart** on page 6, which identifies the specific content skills and process standards found in that activity.

Pretest: The pretest contains a representative sampling of activities similar to those used throughout this book. Give this pretest at one time, or present one problem at a time over a series of days. Students may work on these problems individually, in pairs, or in groups. The purpose of the pretest is to provide insights into the content knowledge and problem-solving strategies students already possess. The emphasis should not be on the number of "right" answers. Instead, encourage students to try their best and write down their ideas. These problems can also provide opportunities for class discussion as students share their thought processes with one another.

0-7424-2884-2 *Using the Standards—Algebra*

Introduction (cont.)

Workbook Pages: Activities can be done independently, in pairs, or in groups. Problems may be broken into parts, with class discussion following student work. Encourage students to create their own strategies for solving the problems. Many activities will lead into subjects that could be investigated or discussed further as a class. You may want to compare different solution methods or discuss how to select a valid solution method for a particular problem. Each activity ends with a **Think** or **Do More** prompt. They are designed as prompts for discussion or journal entries, as jumping off points for further exploration, or as connections to other areas of mathematics.

Create Your Own Problems: At the end of each of the four sections, students will be prompted to create mathematical problems utilizing the concepts learned in that section. You may wish to have students try to solve one another's problems, or even choose some of the student-created problems to be used on a test or for homework.

Check Your Skills: These activities provide a representative sample of the skills developed throughout each section. This can be used as additional practice or as a posttest for the section.

Cumulative Posttest: This is a short posttest providing a representative sample of problems used throughout the book. It may be used for assessment or extra practice. The test can be given all at one time, or may be split up over several days.

Vocabulary Cards: Use the vocabulary cards to familiarize students with mathematical language. The pages may be copied, cut, and pasted onto index cards. Paste the front and back on the same index card to make flash cards, or paste each side on separate cards to use in matching games or activities.

Assessment: Assessment is an integral part of the learning process and can include observations, conversations, interviews, interactive journals, writing prompts, and independent quizzes or tests. Classroom discussions help students learn the difference between poor, good, and excellent responses. Scoring guides can help analyze students' responses. The following is one possible scoring rubric. Modify this rubric as necessary to fit specific problems.

1—Student understands the problem and knows what he is being asked to find.

2—Student selects an appropriate strategy or process to solve the problem.

3—Student is able to model the problem with appropriate manipulatives, graphs, tables, pictures, or computations.

4—Student is able to clearly explain or demonstrate his thinking and reasoning.

0-7424-2884-2 *Using the Standards—Algebra*

NCTM Algebra Standards Correlation Chart

	Problem Solving	Reasoning and Proof	Communication	Connections	Representation
Patterns and Functions					
describe and extend patterns	15–17	14, 18, 20	9–12, 16, 17	10, 11, 13, 19	9–13, 18, 20
represent patterns and functions	26, 27		21–23	25, 28–31	24, 28–31
Situations and Structures					
identify and use properties	40–41	34–37	38–41	34–35, 43–44	40–42
variables	45–46, 52–57	46, 53, 56	45, 50, 57	45–46, 49	47–51, 55–57
equations	60–67	60–63	66–68	58–59, 64–70	58–67
Models					
model with objects and use representations	76–83, 86–87	74–75, 77, 86–87	76–83	74–83, 86–87	74–75, 78–83
Changes in Context					
changes in related variables	86–89	86–87	88–93	86–93	92–93
constant and varying rates of change	94–99	100–101	94–95, 100–105	94–105	96–99, 102

*The pretest, posttest, Create Your Own Problems, and Check Your Skills pages are not included on this chart, but contain a representative sampling of the process standards.

Published by Instructional Fair. Copyright protected.

0-7424-2884-2 *Using the Standards—Algebra*

Pretest

1. Identify the type of pattern (repeating, growing, or decreasing). Then give a rule for the pattern.

a. 15	8	8	15	8	8	_____	_____
b. 7	21	63	189	567	1,701	_____	_____
c. 523	457	391	325	259	193	_____	_____

2. A function machine uses a rule to change numbers. Look for a pattern between the IN and OUT numbers in the table. Fill in the missing numbers. Write the rule.

IN	27		81	36	54	45
OUT		1	9	4		5

Rule: _____

3. Each letter stands for a different number. Find the number that makes each equation true.
   a. $V + 312 = 721$ _____
   b. $T \div 8 = 168$ _____
   c. $45 \times W = 180$ _____
   d. $1,342 - S = 700$ _____

4. There are 30 vehicles in a dealership lot. There are twice as many SUVs as there are cars. There are 8 vans. There is one less truck than there are vans. How many of each type of vehicle is in the lot?

   S = # of SUVs C = # of cars T = # of trucks V = # of Vans
   $S =$ _____ $C =$ _____ $T =$ _____ $V =$ _____

5. A car travels 300 miles at an average speed of 50 miles per hour.
   a. If T is the time it takes for the car to drive 300 miles, write an equation that models this problem.
   b. How long did it take to drive the 300 miles? Show your work. _____

6. Mark used a scale to determine that 3 marbles weigh the same as one block.
   a. If M is the weight of the marble and B is the weight of the block, write an equation showing this relationship.
   b. How many marbles would it take to balance 3 blocks? _____
   c. How many blocks would it take to balance 18 marbles? _____

0-7424-2884-2 *Using the Standards—Algebra*

Pretest (cont.)

7. An object is dropped from the top of the Empire State Building. Which graph shows the relationship between time and the height of the object above the ground? Explain why you chose that graph.

a.

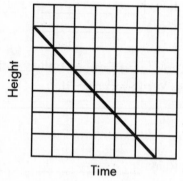

b.

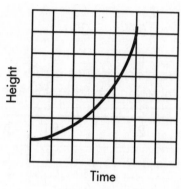

c.

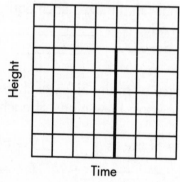

d.

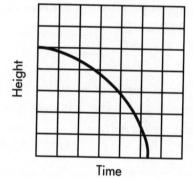

8. A car travels an average speed of 60 miles per hour.

a. Write an equation showing the relationship between the time the car travels, T, and is the distance, D, that it travels.

b. Complete the following table. Show the relationship between the time and the distance traveled.

Time	1		3	4	5		7
Distance		120		240		360	

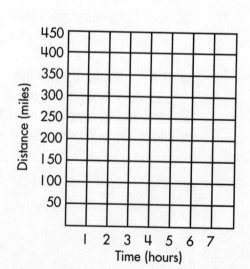

c. Make a graph.

d. Does the distance increase at a constant rate or a varying rate? How do you know?

8

Name _____ Date _____

Doing the Bunny Hop

Ralph Rabbit likes to do the bunny hop. He repeats the same movements over and over to create a **repeating pattern**. For each hopping pattern below, first perform the movements yourself. Then describe the pattern in words. Finally, let each letter A, B, and C stand for a different movement. Use the letters to represent the pattern.

1.

a. Description: _____

b. Letter pattern: _____

2.

a. Description: _____

b. Letter pattern: _____

3.

a. Description: _____

b. Letter pattern: _____

DO MORE

Create your own bunny hop. Make up your own movements and use a repeating pattern. Teach your dance to a friend.

0-7424-2884-2 *Using the Standards—Algebra*

Name _____ Date _____

Polygon Patterns

Find the **repeating pattern**. Draw in the missing shapes. Then describe the pattern using the letters A and B.

1.

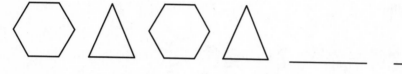

pattern: _____

2.

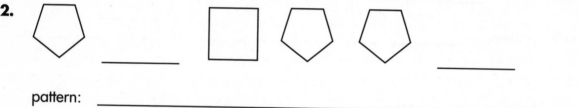

pattern: _____

3.

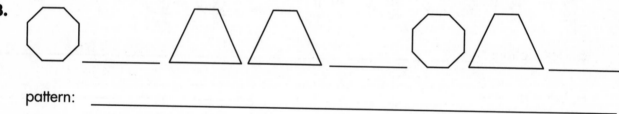

pattern: _____

4.

pattern: _____

DO MORE

Name each of the different polygons used in the patterns above.

0-7424-2884-2 *Using the Standards—Algebra*

Name _____ Date _____

Shape Patterns

Find the **repeating pattern**. Draw in the missing shapes. Then describe the patterns using the letters A and B.

1.

pattern: _____

2.

pattern: _____

3.

pattern: _____

4. How are the three patterns above similar? Explain. _____

_____

_____

DO MORE

Name each of the different shapes used in the patterns above. What do all of these shapes have in common?

0-7424-2884-2 *Using the Standards—Algebra*

Name _____ Date _____

Number Parade

Find the **repeating number pattern**. Insert the missing numbers. Then use letters to show the same pattern. Replace each number with the letter A, B, or C.

1. 5 ____ 4 ____ 9 4 5 ____ ____

Letter pattern: _____

2. ____ 3 6 3 3 ____ ____ 3 6

Letter pattern: _____

3. 1 ____ 2 1 ____ 2 ____ 1 1

Letter pattern: _____

4. 1 5 ____ 7 1 5 5 ____ ____ ____ ____

Letter pattern: _____

5. ____ 2 8 2 ____ 8 ____ ____ ____

Letter pattern: _____

6. 4 ____ 1 4 7 ____ ____ 7 1

Letter pattern: _____

THINK
Look at the patterns above. Are any of the patterns similar? Explain.

0-7424-2884-2 *Using the Standards—Algebra*

Name _____ Date _____

Percussion Patterns

Musical rhythms often contain repeating patterns. Follow the directions below to create your own rhythms.

1. Form groups of 4 people each. Each person should choose an instrument— drums, cymbals, triangle, or maracas. Each person should take a moment to practice playing his or her instrument. If you don't have instruments, be creative. Tap a desk for the drum. Clap your hands for the cymbal. Lightly tap a glass with a pencil for the triangle. Make a "shhhh" sound for the maracas.

2. As a group, choose a letter—A, B, C, or D—to represent each instrument. Choose one of the rhythm patterns below. Each letter of the rhythm pattern stands for one beat from that instrument. Practice "playing" your rhythm by repeating the pattern over and over. Then try the other rhythm patterns.

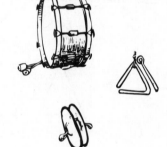

   a. A   B   B

   b. A   B   C   C

   c. A   B   B   C   C   D

   d. A   A   B   C   D

3. Assign each instrument to a letter that is different from the ones you chose in problem 2. Play the rhythm patterns from problem 2 using the new instrument assignments. How does the rhythm sound the same? How is it different?

DO MORE

Create your own rhythm using the four instruments. Write the letter pattern that matches your rhythm. Have your group play the rhythm.

0-7424-2884-2 *Using the Standards—Algebra*

Name _____   Date _____

Pattern Match-Up

For each shape pattern, write the letter of the number pattern that matches it.

_____ 1. ▢ △ △ ▢ △ △

_____ 2. ○ ○ ⏢ ⏢ ○ ○

_____ 3. ☆ ♡ ☆ ♡ ☆ ♡

_____ 4. △ ▢ ⏢ △ ▢ ⏢

A.   0   1   0   1   0   1

B.   1   3   5   1   3   5

C.   3   5   5   3   5   5

D.   2   2   4   4   2   2

THINK

How did you choose matching patterns? Give evidence that shows your answers are right.

0-7424-2884-2 *Using the Standards—Algebra*

Name _____ Date _____

Delightful Designs

Look at each pattern. Answer the questions.

1.

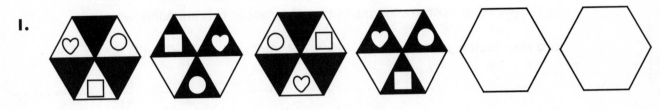

a. How does the shading of the design change from one hexagon to the next?

b. Look at the shapes inside the hexagons. How does the location of the shapes change from one hexagon to the next?

c. Draw the designs for the last two hexagons in the pattern.

2. Dayna drew the following design on a piece of dot paper. Find the pattern she used and complete her drawing.

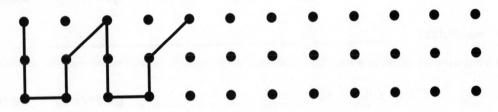

a. How many dots are used to create one cycle of the design? _____

b. How many segments are used to create one cycle of the design? _____

DO MORE

Create your own design that has a pattern. Ask a friend to find the pattern.

0-7424-2884-2 *Using the Standards—Algebra*

Name _____ Date _____

To Grow or Not to Grow

In a **growing pattern**, the numbers get larger in a predictable way.

In a **decreasing pattern**, the numbers get smaller in a predictable way.

Find the pattern. Use the pattern to find the next three numbers in the sequence. Circle either **growing** or **decreasing** to indicate the type of pattern. Then use words to describe how to find the next number in the pattern.

1.   15   26   37   48   ____ ____ ____   **growing**   **decreasing**

Pattern description: _____

2.   950   851   752   653   ____ ____ ____   **growing**   **decreasing**

Pattern description: _____

3.   129   108   87   66   ____ ____ ____   **growing**   **decreasing**

Pattern description: _____

4.   7   88   169   250   331   ____ ____ ____   **growing**   **decreasing**

Pattern description: _____

DO MORE

Create your own pattern. See if a friend can find your pattern.

0-7424-2884-2 *Using the Standards—Algebra*

Name _____ Date _____

Going Up or Coming Down?

In a **growing pattern**, the numbers get larger in a predictable way.

In a **decreasing pattern**, the numbers get smaller in a predictable way.

Find the pattern. Use the pattern to find the next three numbers in the sequence. Circle either **growing** or **decreasing** to indicate the type of pattern. Then use words to describe how to find the next number in the pattern.

1. 5,832   1,944   648   216   ____   ____   ____   **growing**   **decreasing**

Pattern description: _____

2. 8   24   72   216   ____   ____   ____   **growing**   **decreasing**

Pattern description: _____

3. 3   6   12   24   ____   ____   ____   **growing**   **decreasing**

Pattern description: _____

4. 192   96   48   24   ____   ____   ____   **growing**   **decreasing**

Pattern description: _____

THINK

How are patterns 1 and 2 related? How are patterns 3 and 4 related?

0-7424-2884-2 *Using the Standards—Algebra*

Name _____   Date _____

The Case of the Missing Numbers

A **rule** describes the process used to create the pattern.

Example: 10 20 30 40 50   Rule: + 10

Find the patterns. Fill in the missing numbers in the pattern. Write the rule for each pattern.

1. 3   ____   ____   18   23   28   ____   ____

Rule: _____

2. _____   5,000,000   500,000   _____   5,000   500   _____

Rule: _____

3. ____   656   590   524   ____   ____   ____   260

Rule: _____

4. 1.25   ____   ____   80   320   1,280   _____   _____

Rule: _____

DO MORE

Prove that the numbers you chose and your rule work in the pattern. Start with the first number in the pattern. Use your rule to find the next number. Continue until have found 8 numbers. Do these numbers match the ones you found in the problem?

0-7424-2884-2 *Using the Standards—Algebra*

Name _____ Date _____

Rule of Thumb

A **rule** describes the process used to create the pattern.

Example: 1 7 49 343 2,401   Rule: x 7

The first number in the pattern is given. Use the rule to find the next 7 numbers in the pattern.

1. 7 ____ ____ ____ ____ ____ ____ ____

Rule: x 2

2. 896 ____ ____ ____ ____ ____ ____ ____

Rule: ÷ 2

3. 830 ____ ____ ____ ____ ____ ____ ____

Rule: − 111

4. 53 ____ ____ ____ ____ ____ ____ ____

Rule: + 111

THINK

What relationship do you see between patterns 1 and 2? What relationship do you see between patterns 3 and 4?

0-7424-2884-2 *Using the Standards—Algebra*

Name _____ Date _____

Fill in the Blanks

> A **rule** describes the process used to create the pattern.
>
> Example: 63 51 39 27 15   Rule: – 12

Find the patterns. Fill in the missing numbers in the pattern. Write the rule for each pattern.

1. 15   37   59   81   ___   ___   ___   ___

Rule: _____

2. ___   50   42   34   ___   ___   10   ___

Rule: _____

3. 8   30   ___   74   96   ___   ___   ___

Rule: _____

4. ___   ___   47   39   31   ___   ___   7

Rule: _____

THINK

Is the following statement true or false? How do you know?

If two patterns have the same rule, then the patterns will contain the same numbers.

0-7424-2884-2 *Using the Standards—Algebra*

Name _____ Date _____

Keeping It Steady

> If a pattern has a **constant rate**, it changes by the same amount every time.

For each pattern, find the amount of change between each pair of numbers. Then answer the questions.

1. 4   5   7   10   14   19   25   32

a. Is this a growing pattern or a decreasing pattern? _____

b. Does this pattern change at a constant rate? How do you know?

_____

c. Describe the pattern. _____

d. Find the next 3 numbers in the pattern.   _____   _____   _____

2. 29   26   23   20   17   14   11

a. Is this a growing pattern or a decreasing pattern? _____

b. Does this pattern change at a constant rate? How do you know?

_____

c. Describe the pattern. _____

d. Find the next 3 numbers in the pattern.   _____   _____   _____

0-7424-2884-2 *Using the Standards—Algebra*

Name _____ Date _____

Keeping It Steady (cont.)

3. 313   295   279   265   253   243

a. Is this a growing pattern or a decreasing pattern? _____

b. Does this pattern change at a constant rate? How do you know?

_____

c. Describe the pattern. _____

d. Find the next 3 numbers in the pattern. _____ _____ _____

4. 219   220   223   228   235   244

a. Is this a growing pattern or a decreasing pattern? _____

b. Does this pattern change at a constant rate? How do you know?

_____

c. Describe the pattern. _____

d. Find the next 3 numbers in the pattern. _____ _____ _____

DO MORE

Create two patterns of your own. Make one of the patterns change at a constant rate.

0-7424-2884-2 *Using the Standards—Algebra*

Name _____ Date _____

A Tidy Sum

For each pattern, find the amount of change between each pair of numbers. Then answer the questions.

1. 4   5   9   14   23   37   60

    a. Is this a growing pattern or a decreasing pattern? _____

    b. Does this pattern change at a constant rate? How do you know?

    _____

    c. Describe how to find the next number in the pattern. _____

    d. Find the next 3 numbers in the pattern. _____ _____ _____

2. 267   165   102   63   39   24   15

    a. Is this a growing pattern or a decreasing pattern? _____

    b. Does this pattern change at a constant rate? How do you know?

    _____

    c. Describe how to find the next number in the pattern. _____

    d. Find the next 3 numbers in the pattern. _____ _____ _____

THINK

What do these two patterns have in common?

0-7424-2884-2 *Using the Standards—Algebra*

Name _____ Date _____

Function Machine

A **function machine** uses a rule to change numbers. The rule is written on each of the machines. Use the rule to change each of the IN numbers to an OUT number. Write the OUT numbers in the blanks provided.

1.

12   8
5   7
    10

Rule: + 15

— — —

— — —

2.

35
50   44
    21

Rule: – 20

— — —

— — —

3.

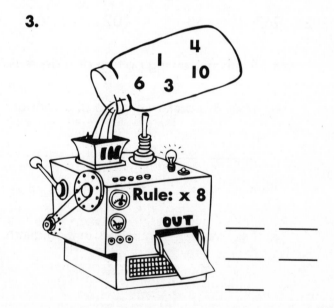

1   4
6   3   10

Rule: x 8

— — —

— — —

DO MORE

Draw your own function machine. Include some IN numbers and some OUT numbers.

0-7424-2884-2 *Using the Standards—Algebra*

Name _____ Date _____

Follow the Rules

A **function machine** uses a rule to change numbers. Use the given rule to change each of the IN numbers to an OUT number.

1.

IN	2	3	6	8	11	14
OUT	9					

Rule: OUT = IN + 7

2.

IN	25	12	35	103	56	81
OUT						

Rule: OUT = IN – 12

3.

IN	15	8	4	21	3	9
OUT						

Rule: OUT = IN x 4

4.

IN	12	48	84	36	90	30
OUT						

Rule: OUT = IN ÷ 6

DO MORE

Create your own rule. Choose some IN numbers. Then use your rule to find the OUT numbers.

0-7424-2884-2 *Using the Standards—Algebra*

Name _____ Date _____

In and Out

A **function machine** uses a rule to change numbers. Look for a pattern between the IN and OUT numbers in each table. Fill in the missing numbers. Write the rule.

1.

IN	3	9	11	6	8
OUT	6		22		16

Rule: _____

2.

IN	4	7	9	44	18
OUT		15	27	52	

Rule: _____

3.

IN	55	38	72	61	80
OUT	26		43		51

Rule: _____

4.

IN	108	27	63	126	18
OUT	12		7		2

Rule: _____

THINK

What method did you use to find the rules? Compare methods with a classmate.

0-7424-2884-2 *Using the Standards—Algebra*

Name _____ Date _____

Function Junction

A **function machine** uses a rule to change numbers. Look for a pattern between the IN and OUT numbers in each table. Fill in the missing numbers. Write the rule.

1.

IN	41	28	110		55	
OUT		13	95	22	40	71

Rule: _____

2.

IN		8		14	5	25
OUT	24	48	54	84	30	

Rule: _____

3.

IN	32	9	22		48	13
OUT		16		72	55	20

Rule: _____

4.

IN	21	28		63	91	
OUT		4	5	9	13	8

Rule: _____

THINK

The rule for a function machine is OUT = IN x 5. The function machine produced an OUT number of 45. What was the IN number? How did you find the answer?

0-7424-2884-2 *Using the Standards—Algebra*

Name _____ Date _____

In a Word

Create a function machine to represent each situation. Tell what the IN and the OUT numbers mean. Write a rule for the function machine. Complete the IN/OUT tables. The first problem has been started for you.

1. Grace has twelve more stickers than Sharon.

IN: number of stickers Sharon has

OUT: number of stickers Grace has

Rule: OUT = IN + 12

IN	0	5	6	11
OUT	12			

2. Miguel eats 3 fewer strawberries than Joe.

IN: _____

OUT: _____

Rule: _____

IN	15	18	22	25
OUT				

3. Darnell has twice as many trading cards as Deshawn.

IN: _____

OUT: _____

Rule: _____

IN	3	7	12	15
OUT				

0-7424-2884-2 *Using the Standards—Algebra*

In a Word (cont.)

4. Lashanda drew four more cartoons than Chu.

IN: _____

OUT: _____

Rule: _____

IN	5	18	12	15
OUT				

5. Kendra got 4 fewer words correct on the spelling test than Chad.

IN: _____

OUT: _____

Rule: _____

IN	17	18	20	31
OUT				

6. Chantelle has 3 times the number of bracelets as Anna.

IN: _____

OUT: _____

Rule: _____

IN	2	4	9	12
OUT				

DO MORE

A function machine has the rule OUT = IN + 5. Make up a situation that the function machine could represent. Use the function machine to create a table of IN and OUT numbers.

Name _____ Date _____

Snow Day

Jamal wants to earn money for a new video game. He decides to charge neighbors $3 to shovel their entryways.

1. How much money will Jamal make if he shovels 2 entries? 5 entries? 7 entries? Show how you found your answers.

2. Write a rule to help Jamal calculate the amount of money he would earn if he shovels 10 entries.

    Money earned = _____

3. Let N stand for the number of entries Jamal shovels. Write a rule that shows how Jamal should calculate the amount of money he would earn if he shoveled N entries.

    Money earned = _____

4. Use the rule to complete the table below, showing how much money Jamal will make shoveling snow.

# of entries	2	5	7	8	10	14
money earned						

0-7424-2884-2 *Using the Standards—Algebra*

Name _____ Date _____

Snow Day (cont.)

5. Make a coordinate graph of the data in the table.

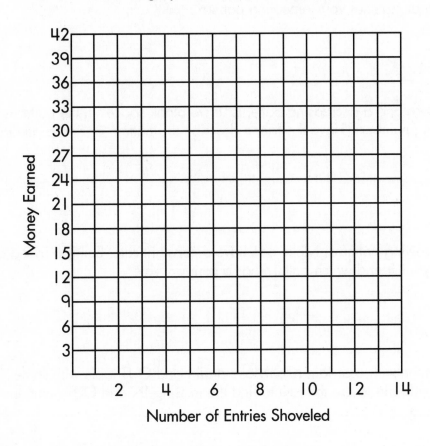

6. Describe any patterns you see in the graph.

DO MORE

The game Jamal wants costs $39. Use the graph to estimate how many entryways Jamal needs to shovel so he can buy the game.

0-7424-2884-2 *Using the Standards—Algebra*

Name _____ Date _____

Create Your Own Problems

1. Create a repeating pattern using shapes, numbers, movements, or rhythms. Have a friend find the letter pattern that matches your repeating pattern.

2. Create a growing pattern and a decreasing pattern. Leave blank spaces in the patterns for a friend to fill in missing numbers. Have the friend describe the pattern or find a rule to fit the pattern.

3. Create two different growing patterns. Make one have a constant rate. See if a friend can find the patterns. Ask your friend which pattern has a constant rate.

4. Create a function machine with a certain rule. Make an IN and OUT table with some missing numbers. Ask a friend to use the rule to find the missing IN and OUT numbers.

5. Make an IN and OUT table that follows a rule. See if your friend can find the rule.

6. Make up a situation and choose some IN numbers. Ask a friend to write the function machine rule that fits the situation and find the OUT numbers.

0-7424-2884-2 *Using the Standards—Algebra*

Name _____ Date _____

Check Your Skills

1. Fill in the missing numbers in the pattern. Identify the type of pattern (repeating, growing, or decreasing). Give a rule for the pattern.

   a. 15   24   33   42   ___   ___   ___

   Type: _____   Rule: _____

   b. 7   7   2   7   ___   ___   ___

   Type: _____   Rule: _____

   c. 178   152   126   100   ___   ___   ___

   Type: _____   Rule: _____

2. Find the next three numbers in each pattern. Describe each of the following patterns. Circle the one(s) that grow at a constant rate.

   a. 3   6   9   15   24   ___   ___   ___

   Pattern: _____

   b. 7   11   15   19   23   ___   ___   ___

   Pattern: _____

3. A function machine uses a rule to change numbers. Look for a pattern between the IN and OUT numbers in the table. Fill in the missing numbers. Write the rule.

IN	3	5		9	10	12
OUT		40	48	72		96

   Rule: _____

    0-7424-2884-2 *Using the Standards—Algebra*

Name _____ Date _____

Marble Mayhem

An operation is **commutative** if changing the order of the numbers does not change the answer.

Answer each of the following questions.

1. Alex put 14 blue marbles into a jar. Then he put 20 red marbles into the jar.
   How many total marbles are in the jar? _____
   Write an equation to represent this situation. _____

2. Alex put 20 red marbles into a jar. Then he put 14 blue marbles into the jar.
   How many total marbles are in the jar? _____
   Write an equation to represent this situation. _____

3. Look at your answers to problems 1 and 2.
   How many total marbles are in each jar? _____ Does it make a difference whether
   Alex puts the red or the blue marbles in the jar first? _____

4. Look at the equations you wrote for problems 1 and 2. What operation (+, −, x, ÷) did you
   use in each equation? _____ Did changing the order of the numbers in the equation
   change the answer? _____

5. Find the answer to each pair of addition problems. What do you notice?

   a. $17 + 8 =$ _____   **b.** $34 + 78 =$ _____
   $8 + 17 =$ _____ $78 + 34 =$ _____

   c. $169 + 243 =$ _____   **d.** $377 + 903 =$ _____
   $243 + 169 =$ _____ $903 + 377 =$ _____

THINK

Is addition **commutative**? Provide reasoning to support your answer.

0-7424-2884-2 *Using the Standards—Algebra*

Name _____ Date _____

Pinching Pennies

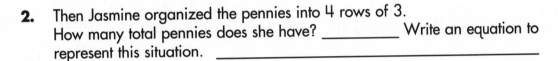

An operation is **commutative** if changing the order of the numbers does not change the answer.

Answer each of the following questions.

1. Jasmine has a bunch of pennies. She organized them into 3 rows of 4. How many total pennies does she have? _____ Write an equation to represent this situation. _____

2. Then Jasmine organized the pennies into 4 rows of 3. How many total pennies does she have? _____ Write an equation to represent this situation. _____

3. Look at your answers to problems 1 and 2. How many total pennies does Jasmine have? _____ Does it make a difference whether she puts the pennies into 3 rows or 4 rows? _____

4. Look at the equations you wrote for problems 1 and 2. What operation (+, −, x, ÷) did you use in each equation? _____ Did changing the order of the numbers in the equation change the answer? _____

5. Find the answer to each pair of addition problems. What do you notice?

   a. 27 x 4 = _____
      4 x 27 = _____

   b. 324 x 8 = _____
      8 x 324 = _____

   c. 169 x 14 = _____
      14 x 169 = _____

   d. 377 x 3 = _____
      3 x 377 = _____

THINK

Is multiplication **commutative**? Provide reasoning to support your answer.

0-7424-2884-2 *Using the Standards—Algebra*

Name _____ Date _____

Groovy Groupings

An operation is **associative** if changing the grouping does not change the answer.

Ms. Jacobson asked her class to solve the following addition problem.

$$7 + 14 + 22$$

Juanita chose to write and solve the problem this way. $(7 + 14) + 22$

$$7 + 14 = 21$$
$$21 + 22 = 43$$

Emily chose to write the problem this way. $7 + (14 + 22)$

1. Show how Emily would solve the problem.

2. What did Emily and Juanita do differently? Did they get the same answer?

3. Rewrite each equation by changing the grouping of the numbers. Then solve each problem.

   a. $33 + (15 + 77) =$ _____ $(33 + 15) + 77 =$ _____

   b. $(126 + 18) + 39 =$ _____   _____ = _____

   c. $(44 + 25) + 430 =$ _____   _____ = _____

   d. $256 + (110 + 568) =$ _____   _____ = _____

4. Is addition associative? Give evidence to support your answer.

DO MORE

Do you think subtraction is associative? How could you test your answer?

0-7424-2884-2 *Using the Standards—Algebra*

Name _____ Date _____

Principled Products

An operation is **associative** if changing the grouping does not change the answer.

Mr. Hernandez asked his class to solve the following multiplication problem.

8 x 4 x 6

José wrote and solved the problem this way. 8 x (4 x 6)

4 x 6 = 24

8 x 24 = 192

Michael wrote the problem this way. (8 x 4) x 6

1. Show how Michael would solve the problem.

2. What did Michael and José do differently? Did they get the same answer?

3. Rewrite each equation by changing the grouping of the numbers. Then solve each problem.

a. 3 x (15 x 2) = _____   (3 x 15) x 2 = _____

b. (6 x 10) x 9 = _____   _____ = _____

c. (4 x 5) x 3 = _____   _____ = _____

d. 25 x (11 x 8) = _____   _____ = _____

4. Is multiplication associative? Give evidence to support your answer.

DO MORE

Do you think division is associative? How could you test your answer?

0-7424-2884-2 *Using the Standards—Algebra*

Name _____ Date _____

Which Property?

An operation is **commutative** if changing the order of the numbers does not change the answer.

$$4 + 8 = 8 + 4$$

$$12 = 12$$

An operation is **associative** if changing the grouping does not change the answer.

$$4 \times (7 \times 6) = (4 \times 7) \times 6$$

$$4 \times 42 = 28 \times 6$$

$$168 = 168$$

Solve both equations to show that they give the same answer. Then write which property, commutative or associative, was used to rewrite the equation.

1. $15 + (87 + 12) =$ $(15 + 87) + 12 =$ _____

2. $27 \times 61 =$ $61 \times 27 =$ _____

3. $(3 \times 16) \times 2 =$ $3 \times (16 \times 2) =$ _____

4. $12 + (82 + 65) =$ $12 + (65 + 82) =$ _____

5. $312 + 77 =$ $77 + 312 =$ _____

6. $75 + (18 + 39) =$ $(75 + 18) + 39 =$ _____

THINK

Explain why you chose commutative or associative for each problem.

0-7424-2884-2 *Using the Standards—Algebra*

Name _____ Date _____

Puzzling Properties

An operation is **commutative** if changing the order of the numbers does not change the answer.

$$4 + 8 = 8 + 4$$

$$12 = 12$$

An operation is **associative** if changing the grouping does not change the answer.

$$4 \times (7 \times 6) = (4 \times 7) \times 6$$

$$4 \times 42 = 28 \times 6$$

$$168 = 168$$

Use the commutative property to rewrite each of the following equations. Check your work by finding the answer to both equations. Make sure the answers are the same.

1. $13 \times 87 =$ _____   _____

2. $183 + 57 =$ _____   _____

3. $79 \times 23 =$ _____   _____

4. $312 + (45 + 38) =$ _____   _____

Use the associative property to rewrite each of the following equations. Check your work by finding the answer to both equations. Make sure the answers are the same.

5. $(22 + 76) + 91 =$ _____   _____

6. $3 \times (14 \times 5) =$ _____   _____

7. $(12 \times 7) \times 2 =$ _____   _____

Name _____ Date _____

Making Models

Sara drew the model below to represent the equation 3 x 4 + 3 x 5.

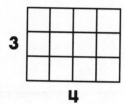

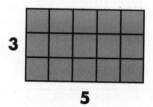

1. What part of the equation represents the number of white squares? _____

2. How many white squares are there? _____

3. What part of the equation represents the number of shaded squares? _____

4. How many shaded squares are there? _____

5. How many total squares are there? _____

6. Solve the equation using arithmetic.

Does your answer match the total number of squares in the model? _____

0-7424-2884-2 *Using the Standards—Algebra*

Name _____ Date _____

Making Models (cont.)

Janelle had an idea for another way to solve this problem. She drew the following model, and wrote this equation. 3 x (4 + 5)

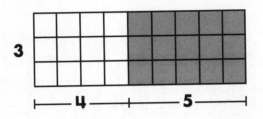

7. Compare Janelle's model to Sarah's model. What do you notice?

8. What does the (4 + 5) in the equation represent on the model?

9. Why does multiplying 3 by (4 + 5) find the total number of squares in the model?

10. Does Janelle's method give the same answer as Sarah's method? Why or why not?

THINK

The **distributive property** says that if you have any three numbers, A, B, and C, then A x B + A x C = A x (B + C). Explain how this property relates to the models Sarah and Janelle drew.

0-7424-2884-2 *Using the Standards—Algebra*

Name _____ Date _____

Model This

The **distributive property** says that if you have any three numbers, A, B, and C, then

$$A \times B + A \times C \qquad = \qquad A \times (B + C).$$

Example: $4 \times 6 + 4 \times 2$ = $4 \times (6 + 2)$

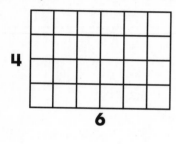   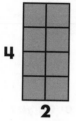

32   =   32

Draw a model to represent each equation below. Use the distributive property to rewrite each of the following equations. Finally, draw a model to represent your new equation.

1. $5 \times 8 + 5 \times 3$

2. $7 \times (2 + 5)$

3. $6 \times 4 + 6 \times 3$

THINK

How cold the distributive property be used to help you do arithmetic?

0-7424-2884-2 *Using the Standards—Algebra*

Name _____ Date _____

Break Down

The **distributive property** says that if you have any three numbers, A, B, and C, then

$$B \times A + C \times A = (B + C) \times A.$$

Trayvon is trying to solve the following multiplication problem. 48 x 7

He decides to break the problem down to make it easier.

First, he puts 48 into expanded form.   48 = 40 + 8

So, his problem now looks like this.   (40 + 8) x 7

He uses the distributive property.   40 x 7 + 8 x 7

He performs the multiplication in his head.   280 + 56

He finds the sum.   336

Solve the following multiplication problems using Trayvon's breakdown method. Show your work.

1. 76 x 3   **2.**   84 x 6

3. 45 x 7   **4.**   98 x 2

5. 29 x 8   **6.**   47 x 9

DO MORE

Check your answers by using a different method to multiply.

0-7424-2884-2 *Using the Standards—Algebra*

Name _____ Date _____

In the Proper Order

To get a correct answer, follow the **order of operations**.

First, do all work in parentheses. Next, do any multiplication or division from left to right.

Finally, do any addition or subtraction from left to right.

Solve each arithmetic problem. Use the correct order of operations.

1. 17 + 3 x (18 – 7)

2. (11 + 14) ÷ 5 + 7

3. (12 – 7) x (33 – 25)

4. 8 + 56 ÷ 7 – 9

5. (7 + 8 – 4) x 5 – 10

6. 19 + 12 ÷ 3 – 6 x 3

DO MORE

Compare your answers with a classmate. If your answers are different, compare your work. Did you use the correct order of operations?

0-7424-2884-2 *Using the Standards—Algebra*

Name _____ Date _____

Digit Dilemma

Read the clues about each number to find its missing digit(s).

1. ____ ____ 4

I am a 3-digit number between 200 and 400. I am divisible by 4.
The sum of my digits is 13.

2. 7 ____ ____

Each of my digits is prime and the sum of my digits is prime. The digit in the
tens place is less than the digit in the ones place.

3. 4 ____ 1 ____

I am a 4-digit number. I am divisible by 5. The sum of my digits is 15.

4. ____ 0 ____

I am an odd number greater than 500. The sum of my digits is 11.

THINK

Discuss your strategies with a classmate. How did you find the right answer?

0-7424-2884-2 *Using the Standards—Algebra*

Name _____ Date _____

Number Clues

Read the clues. Find the number.

1. _____, _____ _____ _____

   I am a 4-digit number larger than 2,500. No two of my digits are the same.
   The product of the thousands digit and the hundreds digit is equal to the ones digit.
   The sum of my digits is 16.

2. _____, _____ _____ _____

   I am a 4-digit number greater than 5,000. The sum of my digits is 15. My tens digit
   is three times greater than my ones digit. My thousands digit is one greater than my
   tens digit.

3. _____ _____, _____ _____ _____

   I am a 5-digit number. My ones digit is three times greater than my tens digit. My
   ten-thousand digit is 3 more than my tens digit. My hundreds digit is twice my
   ten-thousand digit. My thousands digit is one less than my hundreds digit.

4. _____ _____, _____ _____ _____

   I am a 5-digit number between 52,000 and 53,000. The sum of my digits is 21.
   My ones digit is a multiple of 3. My tens digit is equal to my hundreds digit.

THINK

Is there only one answer to each of the puzzles? How do you know?

0-7424-2884-2 *Using the Standards—Algebra*

Name _____ Date _____

Mystery Numbers

Each symbol below represents a different number. Some of the numbers are known, but others are a mystery. Use the equations to help find the mystery numbers.

1. △ = 2   ♡ = 7

    ♡ − △ = ☆   ☆ = _____

2. ♣ = 3

    ♣ × ☆ = ◇   ◇ = _____

3. ○ = 6

    ◇ − ○ = ▢   ▢ = _____

4. ➤ = 4

    ➤ × ♣ = 🌼   🌼 = _____

5. 🌼 ÷ ○ + ▢ = ☾   ☾ = _____

DO MORE

Use these symbols to make up your own equations. Make up your own symbols to represent other numbers. See if a friend can find your mystery numbers.

0-7424-2884-2 *Using the Standards—Algebra*

Name _____ Date _____

Missing Numbers

Each letter below represents a different number. Some of the numbers are known, but the others are missing. Use the equations to find the missing numbers.

$n = 8$ $t = 24$ $f = 30$ $r = 16$

$p = 18$ $j = 3$ $b = 5$ $e = 4$

$n + j = y$ $f \div b = c$ $b \times e = k$ $r \div n = a$

$a + b = s$ $t + r = g$ $g - s = d$ $r \times a = h$

$h - c = m$ $m \div a = z$ $r + p - s = v$ $g - e \times j = w$

1. $y = $ _____   **2.** $c = $ _____   **3.** $k = $ _____   **4.** $a = $ _____

5. $s = $ _____   **6.** $g = $ _____   **7.** $d = $ _____   **8.** $h = $ _____

9. $m = $ _____   **10.** $z = $ _____   **11.** $v = $ _____   **12.** $w = $ _____

THINK
What happens if you choose the wrong number for one of the letters? How will this affect the rest of your answers?

0-7424-2884-2 *Using the Standards—Algebra*

Name _____ Date _____

Solve It!

A **variable** is a letter or symbol that stands for an unknown number.

Use the inverse operation to find the value of each variable. The first few problems have been started for you.

1. $13 + \heartsuit = 27$

$27 - 13 = \heartsuit$

$\heartsuit = $ _____

2. $L \div 3 = 28$

$28 \times 3 = L$

$L = $ _____

3. $\clubsuit \times 7 = 84$

$84 \div 7 = \clubsuit$

$\clubsuit = $ _____

4. $T - 42 = 13$

$T = $ _____

5. $\newmoon + 73 = 111$

$\newmoon = $ _____

6. $66 - P = 45$

$P = $ _____

DO MORE

Create your own equation with a variable. See if a classmate can find the value of the variable.

0-7424-2884-2 *Using the Standards—Algebra*

Name _____ Date _____

Valuable Variables

A **variable** is a letter or symbol that stands for an unknown number.

Find the value of each variable that makes the equation true.

I. $513 + $ ⭐ $= 275$

⭐ $= $ _____

2. $M \div 18 = 3$

$M = $ _____

3. $27 \times $ △ $= 594$

△ $= $ _____

4. $P - 1,288 = 977$

$P = $ _____

5. ⬡ $+ 673 = 8,541$

⬡ $= $ _____

6. $676 - R = 355$

$R = $ _____

7. ➡ $\div 12 = 132$

➡ $= $ _____

8. $V \times 15 = 345$

$V = $ _____

THINK

Explain the strategies you used to find the value of the variables.

0-7424-2884-2 *Using the Standards—Algebra*

Name _____ Date _____

Solution Pairs

A **variable** is a letter or symbol that stands for an unknown number. If there are two variables in an equation, there are many different pairs of numbers that make the equation true.

Example: $t + v = 7$

$3 + 4 = 7$ $t = 3$ $v = 4$

$2 + 5 = 7$ $t = 2$ $v = 5$

For each equation, find the missing number that completes each pair.

1. $m \times 4 = p$

    a. $m = 3$ $p =$ _____

    b. $m =$ _____ $p = 8$

    c. $m = 9$ $p =$ _____

2. $h - 12 = j$

    a. $h = 15$ $j =$ _____

    b. $h = 25$ $j =$ _____

    c. $h =$ _____ $j = 8$

3. $r + s = 13$

    a. $r = 1$ $s =$ _____

    b. $r = 9$ $s =$ _____

    c. $r = 4$ $s =$ _____

4. $24 \div d = f$

    a. $d =$ _____ $f = 6$

    b. $d = 3$ $f =$ _____

    c. $d =$ _____ $f = 12$

DO MORE

For each equation above, find another pair that makes the equation true.

       0-7424-2884-2 *Using the Standards—Algebra*

Name _____ Date _____

A Sporting Chance

David, Juan, Terell, and Andrew like to collect and trade sports cards. How many cards does each boy have? Use the clues to find the answer.

1. All together, the boys have 100 cards. Juan has 32 cards. Andrew has half as many cards as Juan. David and Terell have the same number of cards.

    D = David's total number of cards $D =$ _____

    J = Juan's total number of cards $J =$ _____

    T = Terell's total number of cards $T =$ _____

    A = Andrew's total number of cards $A =$ _____

Each boy has some combination of football, baseball, and hockey cards. How many cards of each type do the boys have? Use the clues to find the answers.

F = number of football cards H = number of hockey cards B = number of baseball cards

2. Juan has 14 football cards. He has twice as many baseball cards as hockey cards.

    $F =$ _____ $B =$ _____ $H =$ _____

3. Half of Andrew's cards are hockey cards. He has 2 more baseball cards than football cards.

    $F =$ _____ $B =$ _____ $H =$ _____

4. David only has 1 baseball card. He has 5 fewer hockey cards than football cards.

    $F =$ _____ $B =$ _____ $H =$ _____

5. Terell has 9 hockey cards. He has 3 more baseball cards than football cards.

    $F =$ _____ $B =$ _____ $H =$ _____

THINK

What strategies did you use to solve the problems?

0-7424-2884-2 *Using the Standards—Algebra*

A Baker's Dozen

Some of Mr. Baker's students are baking cookies to sell at the school carnival. They have chocolate chip, sugar, peanut butter, and oatmeal raisin cookies. How many of each type did his students bring? Use the clues to find the answers.

C = number of chocolate chip cookies   S = number of sugar cookies

P = number of peanut butter cookies   O = number of oatmeal raisin cookies

1. Jessica brought 3 dozen cookies. She brought 15 chocolate chip cookies. She brought the same number of sugar, peanut butter, and oatmeal cookies.

    C = _____   S = _____   P = _____   O = _____

2. Carlos brought 60 cookies. He brought a dozen oatmeal raisin cookies. He brought twice as many chocolate chip cookies as peanut butter cookies. He brought 8 more chocolate chip cookies than oatmeal raisin cookies.

    C = _____   S = _____   P = _____   O = _____

3. Kanisha brought 100 cookies. Half of the cookies she brought were peanut butter. Half of the remaining cookies were sugar. There were 5 more chocolate chip cookies than oatmeal raisin cookies.

    C = _____   S = _____   P = _____   O = _____

4. Daniel brought 4 dozen cookies. He brought 20 oatmeal raisin cookies. He brought 8 fewer sugar cookies than oatmeal raisin cookies. He brought 10 more peanut butter cookies than chocolate chip cookies.

    C = _____   S = _____   P = _____   O = _____

THINK

How can you prove that your solutions are correct?

0-7424-2884-2 *Using the Standards—Algebra*

Name _____ Date _____

Nature Walk

Ms. Bailey, the camp counselor, asked her campers to keep their eyes open for wildlife during their nature walks. They kept a tally of the number of animals they saw each day. How many of each type of animals did they see? Use the clues to find the answers.

B = number of birds S = number of squirrels C = number of chipmunks

R = number of rabbits D = number of deer N = number of raccoons

1. On Monday morning, the campers saw 21 animals: birds, squirrels, and deer. They saw 5 deer. They saw three times as many birds as squirrels.

   B = _____ S = _____ D = _____

2. On Tuesday afternoon, the campers saw 30 animals. They saw 14 birds. They saw 6 fewer squirrels than birds. They saw three times as many chipmunks as rabbits. They didn't see any deer or raccoons.

   B = _____ S = _____ R = _____ C = _____

3. On Wednesday evening, the campers saw 18 animals. They saw 4 deer. They saw two more raccoons than deer. They saw the same number of birds as rabbits. They saw $\frac{1}{3}$ as many squirrels as raccoons.

   B = _____ S = _____ D = _____ R = _____ N = _____

4. On Friday, the campers saw a record of 40 animals. Half the animals they saw were birds. They saw $\frac{1}{4}$ as many chipmunks as birds. They saw only 1 squirrel. They saw twice as many rabbits as they saw raccoons. They saw twice as many deer as they saw rabbits.

   B = _____ S = _____ C = _____

   R = _____ D = _____ N = _____

DO MORE

Make up your own number clues to fit this situation. See if a classmate can find the number of each animal.

54

        0-7424-2884-2 *Using the Standards—Algebra*

Name _____ Date _____

Symbol Sense

Each symbol stands for a number. Find the numbers that will make both equations true.

1. △ + ☐ = 11

△ × ☐ = 30

△ = ___   ☐ = ___

2. ⬡ × ▭ = 24

⬡ − ▭ = 10

⬡ = ___   ▭ = ___

3. 🌼 + 🕷 = 15

🌼 × 🕷 = 56

🌼 = ___   🕷 = ___

4. ➡ − ☆ = 21

➡ × ☆ = 100

➡ = ___   ☆ = ___

5. ☾ × ⬭ = 100

☾ + ⬭ = 25

☾ = ___   ⬭ = ___

6. ⬯ − ◇ = 5

⬯ × ◇ = 36

⬯ = ___   ◇ = ___

THINK

Here are two different strategies for solving these problems:

1. Find pairs of numbers that have the correct sum (or difference) and then see which of these have the correct product.

2. Find pairs of numbers that have the correct product and then see which of these have the correct sum (or difference).

Which is the most efficient way to solve these problems?

0-7424-2884-2 *Using the Standards—Algebra*

Name _____ Date _____

Alphabet Soup

In each problem, different letters stand for different numbers. Find the numbers that will make both equations true.

1. $W + Y = 8$

$3 \times Y = 18$

$W =$ _____ $Y =$ _____

2. $80 \div B = C$

$6 + C = 10$

$B =$ _____ $C =$ _____

3. $7 + K = 12$

$2 \times K = L$

$K =$ _____ $L =$ _____

4. $M - N = 22$

$M + 12 = 52$

$M =$ _____ $N =$ _____

5. $D + F = 25$

$F \div 3 = 6$

$D =$ _____ $F =$ _____

6. $5 \times P = Q$

$P + Q = 24$

$P =$ _____ $Q =$ _____

7. $48 \div T = 16$

$T \times V = 15$

$T =$ _____ $V =$ _____

8. $H + 14 = 30$

$J - H = 9$

$J =$ _____ $H =$ _____

DO MORE

How can you prove that your answers are correct?

0-7424-2884-2 *Using the Standards—Algebra*

Name _____ Date _____

Triple Tease

For each problem below, different shapes represent different numbers. Find the numbers for each shape that make all three equations true.

1. ⬡ + ⬡ = 16

△ x 3 = ▭

▭ − ⬡ = 7

△ = _____

▭ = _____

⬡ = _____

2. ◇ + ◯ = 15

◇ x ☆ = 30

◯ − 7 = 2

◯ = _____

◇ = _____

☆ = _____

3. ⬠ x 4 = ▢

▢ + ◗ = 17

14 ÷ ⬠ = 7

⬠ = _____

◗ = _____

▢ = _____

4. ⬆ − ▱ = 3

⬆ + 8 = ◖

◖ ÷ 2 = 6

⬆ = _____

▱ = _____

◖ = _____

DO MORE

Discuss the strategies you used to solve these problems with a classmate.

0-7424-2884-2 *Using the Standards—Algebra*

Exceptional Equations

A **variable** is a letter or symbol that stands for an unknown number. If there are two variables in an equation, there are many different pairs of numbers that make the equation true.

1. Josh and Hasheem like to play basketball. Yesterday, Josh shot 4 more baskets than Hasheem. Josh shot *J* baskets and Hasheem shot *H* baskets.

   a. Write an equation showing this relationship.

   b. If Hasheem shot 12 baskets, how many did Josh shoot?

     H = _____   *J* = _____

   c. If Josh shot 12 baskets, how many did Hasheem shoot?

     H = _____   *J* = _____

2. Kashana is helping her older sister run for class president. She is making campaign buttons. She made 16 fewer buttons yesterday than she did today. She made *Y* buttons yesterday and *T* buttons today.

   a. Write an equation showing this relationship.

   b. If Kashana made 55 buttons today, how many did she make yesterday?

     Y = _____   *T* = _____

   c. If Kashana made 60 buttons yesterday, how many did she make today?

     Y = _____   *T* = _____

0-7424-2884-2 *Using the Standards—Algebra*

Name _____ Date _____

Exceptional Equations (cont.)

3. Antonio is organizing his comic collection into boxes. Each box holds 15 comics. Josh has N boxes and a total of T comics.

a. Write an equation showing this relationship.

b. If Antonio has 6 full boxes, how many total comics does he have?

N = _____   T = _____

c. If Antonio has 120 comics, how many boxes does he need?

N = _____   T = _____

4. The fourth-grade classes are going on a field trip. Each bus is full and holds 32 people. There are B buses and P people on the trip.

a. Write an equation showing this relationship.

b. If there are 4 buses, how many people are going on the trip?

B = _____   P = _____

c. If there are 192 people, how many buses are there?

B = _____   P = _____

DO MORE

For each of the problems, find three more pairs of numbers that would work in the equations. Tell what the numbers mean in that situation.

0-7424-2884-2 *Using the Standards—Algebra*

Name _____ Date _____

That's a Puzzler

Equations are often used to help solve problems. A **variable** is a letter that represents the amount you are trying to find. Follow the steps to help solve this word problem:

Hannah is almost finished putting together a 500-piece puzzle. She counted 114 pieces still in the box. How many pieces has she already put together?

1. Use N as the variable in this problem. What should N represent?

$N =$ _____

2. The following word equation describes the relationship between the known and unknown values in the problem. Replace the words with numbers or variables to create a mathematical equation.

\# of pieces in the box + \# of pieces put together = total \# of pieces in puzzle

3. Find the value of N that makes this equation true. Show how you found your answer.

4. In word problems, you should always write your answer in a complete sentence that relates back to the original problem. Complete the following sentence.

Hannah has put together _____ pieces of the puzzle.

DO MORE

How can you show that your answer is correct?

0-7424-2884-2 *Using the Standards—Algebra*

Name _____ Date _____

Picture Perfect

Equations are often used to help solve problems. A **variable** is a letter that represents the amount you are trying to find. Follow the steps to help solve this word problem:

Justin bought a new digital camera so that he doesn't have to carry around bulky rolls of film. A roll of film holds 24 pictures. The memory card on the camera holds 360 pictures. How many rolls of film does the memory card replace?

1. Use *R* as the variable in this problem. What should *R* represent?

R = _____

2. Use words to write an equation describing the relationship between the known and unknown values in the problem.

3. Replace the words in the sentence above with numbers and variables to make a mathematical equation.

4. Find the value of *R* that makes this equation true. Show how you found your answer.

5. In word problems, you should always write your answer in a complete sentence that relates back to the original problem. Complete the following sentence.

The memory card replaces _____ rolls of film.

DO MORE

How can you show that your answer is correct?

0-7424-2884-2 *Using the Standards—Algebra*

Name _____ Date _____

A Sweet Treat

Equations are often used to help solve problems. A **variable** is a letter that represents the amount you are trying to find. Follow the steps to help solve this word problem:

Tranice brought a bag full of candy to her class party. The bag held 250 miniature candy bars. When Tranice got home, there were 75 candy bars left in the bag. How many candy bars did the class eat?

1. Use B as the variable in this problem. What should B represent?

$B =$ _____

2. Use words to write an equation describing the relationship between the known and unknown values in the problem.

3. Replace the words in the sentence above with numbers and variables to make a mathematical equation.

4. Find the value of B that makes this equation true. Show how you found your answer.

5. In word problems, you should always write your answer in a complete sentence that relates back to the original problem. Complete the following sentence.

The class ate _____ candy bars.

DO MORE

How can you show that your answer is correct?

Name _____ Date _____

Taking a Trip

Equations are often used to help solve problems. A **variable** is a letter that represents the amount you are trying to find. Follow the steps to help solve this word problem:

The fourth-grade classes are going on a field trip to the Science and Industry Museum. There are 75 students going on the trip. A chaperone is needed for every 5 students. How many chaperones are needed for the trip?

1. Use C as the variable in this problem. What should C represent?

$C =$ _____

2. Use words to write an equation describing the relationship between the known and unknown values in the problem.

3. Replace the words in the sentence above with numbers and variables to make a mathematical equation.

4. Find the value of C that makes this equation true. Show how you found your answer.

5. In word problems, you should always write your answer in a complete sentence that relates back to the original problem. Complete the following sentence.

They will need _____ chaperones on the trip.

DO MORE

How can you show that your answer is correct?

0-7424-2884-2 *Using the Standards—Algebra*

Name _____ Date _____

Finding Unknowns

Equations are often used to help solve problems. A **variable** is a letter that represents an unknown amount. Follow the directions to help you solve each word problem.

1. Carlita is helping her mother set up the school cafeteria for the PTA potluck dinner. They are expecting 108 people. Each round table holds 6 people. How many tables will they need?

    a. Choose a letter to use for a variable and explain what the variable represents.

    b. Write an equation that models the problem.

    c. Solve the problem. Show your work. Write your answer in a complete sentence.

2. Bai enjoys bicycling. Last summer, he bought a new bike. He needs to give the bike a tune-up once it has been ridden 1,000 miles. So far, he has ridden a total of 438 miles. How many more miles can he ride before his bike needs a tune-up?

    a. Choose a letter to use for a variable and explain what the variable represents.

    b. Write an equation that models the problem.

    c. Solve the problem. Show your work. Write your answer in a complete sentence.

     0-7424-2884-2 *Using the Standards—Algebra*

Name _____ Date _____

Finding Unknowns (cont.)

3. Elizabeth has a large coin collection. She keeps all 1,060 of her coins in a large binder. 53 special pages in the binder hold coins. How many coins does each page hold?

   a. Choose a letter to use for a variable and explain what the variable represents.

   b. Write an equation that models the problem.

   c. Solve the problem. Show your work. Write your answer in a complete sentence.

4. Kevin is planting tulip bulbs in the flower garden. He has a total of 72 bulbs to plant. After he has been working for a couple of hours, he counts 28 bulbs remaining in the bag. How many bulbs has he planted so far?

   a. Choose a letter to use for a variable and explain what the variable represents.

   b. Write an equation that models the problem.

   c. Solve the problem. Show your work. Write your answer in a complete sentence.

THINK

How can writing equations help you solve problems?

0-7424-2884-2 *Using the Standards—Algebra*

Name _____ Date _____

Perplexing Problems

Equations are often used to help solve problems. A **variable** is a letter that represents an unknown amount. Follow the directions to help you solve each word problem.

1. Christopher and Rayshon are the best soccer players on their team. Christopher scored *C* goals and Rayshon scored *R* goals.

    a. This year they scored a combined total of 18 goals. Write an equation showing this relationship.

    b. Christopher scored 8 more goals than Rayshon. Write an equation showing this relationship.

    c. How many goals did each of the boys score? Explain how you found your answer.

    C = _____   *R* = _____

2. Akina is selling ice-cream cones in her dad's store. She sold *H* Chocolate cones and *V* vanilla cones.

    a. Today she sold 20 chocolate and vanilla cones. Write an equation showing this relationship.

    b. She sold 8 fewer vanilla cones than she did chocolate. Write an equation showing this relationship.

    c. How many of each type of ice cream did Akina sell? Explain how you found your answer.

    H = _____   *V* = _____

0-7424-2884-2 *Using the Standards—Algebra*

Perplexing Problems (cont.)

3. Kyeesha likes to put together models. She has 18 models all together: *A* model airplanes, *S* model ships, and *T* model trucks.

    a. One-third of the models Kyeesha owns are airplanes. Write an equation showing this relationship.

    b. Kyeesha has a total of 10 model airplanes and ships combined. Write an equation showing this relationship.

    c. How many airplanes, ships, and trucks does Kyeesha have? Show your work.

    $A =$ _____ $S =$ _____ $T =$ _____

4. James decided to make some money babysitting. He charges $6 an hour.

    a. On Friday he made *F* dollars and on Saturday he made *S* dollars. He made $54 all together. Write an equation showing this relationship.

    b. He worked for 4 hours on Friday and made *F* dollars. Write an equation showing this relationship.

    c. How much money did James make each day? Show your work.

    $F =$ _____ $S =$ _____

THINK
Could you have solved these problems with only one equation? Why or why not?

0-7424-2884-2 *Using the Standards—Algebra*

Name _____ Date _____

How Far?

This equation can help you find the distance an object travels if it moves at a constant speed for a certain amount of time.

$$D = R \times T$$

D = distance traveled R = rate (or speed) T = time

---

1. Thanh and his family are driving to an amusement park. It took them 5 hours to get there. They averaged 60 miles per hour. How far away is the amusement park? Write an equation and show your work.

2. Megan and her father rode their bikes to the ice-cream store. They averaged 12 miles per hour. It took them 2 hours of riding time to get to the store. How far away is the store? Write an equation and show your work.

3. Alex took a direct flight on a 747 jet to visit his grandparents. When the flight ended 4 hours later, the captain said they had averaged 570 miles per hour. How far away do his grandparents live? Write an equation and show your work.

4. Gracia took a bus tour. The bus averaged 40 miles per hour and the tour lasted 3 hours. How far did the bus travel? Write an equation and show your work.

THINK

Explain how you might use the distance equation in your life.

0-7424-2884-2 *Using the Standards—Algebra*

Name _____ Date _____

How Fast?

This equation can help you find the distance an object travels if it
moves at a constant speed for a certain amount of time.

$$D = R \times T$$

D = distance traveled R = rate (or speed) T = time

1. Teandre walked 8 km in 4 hours. How fast did he walk? Write an equation and
   show your work.

2. Kayla likes to jog. It took her 1.25 hours to jog 5 miles around the track. What was her
   average speed? Write an equation and show your work.

3. Alejandro and his family are going on a cross-country trip. The first day, they drove
   420 miles. They spent 7 hours driving in the car. What was their average speed?
   Write an equation and show your work.

4. Lien bikes 36 miles on a trail. It takes her 3 hours. What was her average speed? Write
   an equation and show your work.

DO MORE

Write an equation that shows how to find the rate if you know the distance and the time. How is
this equation related to the distance equation given at the top of the page? $R =$ _____

0-7424-2884-2 *Using the Standards—Algebra*

Name _____ Date _____

How Long?

> This equation can help you find the distance an object travels if it moves at a constant speed for a certain amount of time.
>
> $$D = R \times T$$
>
> D = distance traveled R = rate (or speed) T = time

1. A 747 jet flies 500 miles per hour for a distance of 1,500 miles. How long did the trip take? Write an equation and show your work.

2. Jason biked 60 miles. He averaged 15 miles per hour. How long did he ride? Write an equation and show your work.

3. Rachel jogged 5 miles to the store. She averaged 3 miles per hour. How long did it take her to get to the store? Write an equation and show your work.

4. Raúl rode the bus to visit his uncle in another city 195 miles away. The bus averaged 65 miles per hour. How long did the trip take? Write an equation and show your work.

DO MORE

Write an equation that shows how to find the time if you know the distance and the rate. How is this equation related to the distance equation given at the top of the page? $T =$ _____

Name _____ Date _____

Create Your Own Problems

1. Write 3 different addition or multiplication equations. Then rewrite each equation using the commutative or associative property. Ask a classmate to figure out which property was used to rewrite the equation.

2. Write 4 equations: one with addition, one with subtraction, one with multiplication, and one with division. Each equation should have one unknown value. Use a different symbol to represent each unknown value. Have a classmate solve your equations.

3. Choose two numbers between 2 and 10. Find their product and then find their sum. Now, choose a different symbol to represent each of the numbers. Use the product and sum to write two equations using the symbols. See if a classmate can use the equations to find your two numbers.

4. Make up a story problem with two unknown amounts. Tell how the amounts are related to each other. Choose a letter to represent each variable. Have a classmate write an equation that models the problem. Give an amount for one of the variables and have your classmate find the value of the other variable.

5. Make up a story problem involving distance, rate, and time. Give two out of the three measurements and have a classmate find the third measurement.

Name _____ Date _____

Check Your Skills

1. Use either the commutative, associative, or distributive property to rewrite each equation in an equivalent form. Tell which property you used.

a. $(7 + 9) + 12 =$ _____ _____

b. $6 \times (15 + 32) =$ _____ _____

c. $3 \times 26 =$ _____ _____

2. I am an even 4-digit number greater than 5,000. The sum of my digits is 9. The hundreds digit is greater than the tens digit, but less than the ones digit. What number am I? _____

3. Each symbol stands for a different number. Find the number that makes each equation true.

a. $571 +$ ♣ $= 1,062$

♣ = _____

b. $18 \times$ ☾ $= 90$

☾ = _____

c. $192 \div$ ★ $= 12$

★ = _____

d. $931 -$ ◇ $= 768$

◇ = _____

4. Three children are making snowballs for a snowball fight. All together, they have made 45 snowballs. Mara has made twice as many as Christian. Vickie has made 15. How many did each child make?

$M =$ _____ $C =$ _____ $V =$ _____

0-7424-2884-2 *Using the Standards—Algebra*

Name _____ Date _____

Check Your Skills

5. Each letter stands for a number. Find the numbers that make both equations true.

a. $B + D = 18$

$B \times D = 45$

$B =$ _____

$D =$ _____

b. $T - R = 8$

$84 \div T = 7$

$R =$ _____

$T =$ _____

6. Denisha and Amanda are selling candy bars as a school fundraiser. Amanda sold 23 fewer bars than Denisha.

a. Amanda sold A bars and Denisha sold D bars. Write an equation showing this relationship.

b. If Denisha sold 60 bars, how many did Amanda sell?

$D =$ _____ $A =$ _____

c. If Amanda sold 30 bars, how many did Denisha sell?

$D =$ _____ $A =$ _____

7. A car travels 280 miles in 4 hours.

a. Write an equation that models this problem if R is the speed the car was traveling.

b. How fast was the car traveling? Show your work.

$R =$ _____

0-7424-2884-2 *Using the Standards—Algebra*

Name _____ Date _____

Weighty Matters

Materials: balance, pennies, quarters, dimes

Complete the following experiments to compare the weights of pennies, dimes, and quarters.

1. Use a balance scale. Place a quarter on one side of the scale. Place a penny on the other side of the scale. Which is heavier? _____

2. Keep adding pennies and/or quarters until the scale is balanced. Let P = the weight of a penny. Let Q = the weight of a quarter. Write an equation that shows the relationship between the weight of a penny and the weight of a quarter.

    _____

3. Use your equation from question 2 to predict the answers to the following questions. Show how you got your answers.

    a. How many pennies would it take to balance 2 quarters? _____

    b. How many quarters would it take to balance 8 pennies? _____

    c. How many pennies would it take to balance 6 quarters? _____

4. Use the scale to test your answers to question 3. Were you correct? _____

5. Remove the coins from the balance scale. Now place a penny on one side and a dime on the other side. Which is heavier? _____

74

Name _____ Date _____

Weighty Matters (cont.)

6. Keep adding pennies and dimes until the scale is balanced. Let P = the weight of a penny. Let D = the weight of a dime. Write an equation that shows the relationship between the weight of a penny and the weight of a dime.

_____

7. Use your equation from question 6 to predict the answers to the following questions. Show how you got your answers.

   a. How many pennies would it take to balance 10 dimes? _____

   b. How many dimes would it take to balance 12 pennies? _____

   c. How many pennies would it take to balance 20 dimes? _____

8. Use the scale to test your answers to question 7. Were you correct? _____

9. Use the equations you have made to predict how many dimes and quarters will balance out the scale. Show how you got your answer.

10. Use the scale to test your answer to question 9. Were you correct? _____

DO MORE

Use a balance scale to determine how many nickels and pennies it will take to balance the scale.

0-7424-2884-2 *Using the Standards—Algebra*

Name _____ Date _____

Container Calculations

Materials: cylinder (example: oatmeal container)
square prism (example: box that held gallon-size plastic storage bags)
marbles

1. Look at the two containers. Which one do you think is the larger container? Explain your reasoning.

2. Fill each of the containers with marbles. Count the number of marbles that fit inside each container. Which container holds the most marbles?

_____

3. Was your prediction correct? Why do you think this is the case?

0-7424-2884-2 *Using the Standards—Algebra*

Name _____   Date _____

Container Calculations (cont.)

Filling each container takes a lot of time. Using mathematical equations could help you find the answer much quicker. To find the **volume** of a cylinder or prism, multiply the area of the base by the height.

4. Write an equation for finding the area of a square with a side length of *s*.

A = _____

5. Now write an equation for finding the volume of a square prism with a height of *H*.

V = _____

6. An equation for finding the area of a circle is $A = 3.14 \times r^2$, where *r* is the radius of the circle. Write an equation for finding the volume of a cylinder with a height of *h*.

V = _____

7. Measure the dimensions of each container in centimeters.

Square Prism
side length = _____
height = _____

Cylinder
radius = _____
height = _____

8. Find the volume of each container. Show your work.

Square Prism: V = _____

Cylinder: V = _____

DO MORE

A container shaped like a square prism and a container shaped like a cylinder both have a height of 8 cm. The prism has a base with side lengths of 4 cm. The cylinder has a base with a diameter of 4 cm. Which container will hold more? Explain your reasoning.

0-7424-2884-2 *Using the Standards—Algebra*

Name _____ Date _____

Recreational Rectangles

Materials: uncooked spaghetti noodles, ruler

Mr. Jones just bought 24 yards of fencing to make a pen for his dog. He will make the pen in the shape of a rectangle. The fencing comes in 1-yard sections. What are all the different dimensions his yard could have?

1. Use uncooked spaghetti noodles to model this situation. The noodles will model the fencing, with each 1 centimeter representing 1 yard of fencing. Cut several strands of noodles into pieces that are 24 cm long. Discard remaining noodle parts.

2. Find the length of the pen if Mr. Jones decided to make the width 1 foot long. Experiment with 24-cm length noodles. Cut two 1-inch pieces off the noodle. These will be the sides of the rectangle.

   a. How long is the piece of noodle you have left? _____

   b. How would you cut the remaining piece of noodle to create the top and bottom of the rectangle?

   c. What is the length of this rectangle?

   W = 1 cm   L = _____ cm

3. Make a table showing the length of each rectangular pen with the following widths. Use the strands of 24-cm spaghetti noodles to help you find the correct lengths.

width (cm)	1	2	3	4	5	6	7	8	9
length (cm)									

0-7424-2884-2 *Using the Standards—Algebra*

Recreational Rectangles (cont.)

4. How many differently-sized rectangles can Mr. Jones make? Expand the table from problem 3 if necessary. Then explain your answer.

5. Explain any shortcuts or strategies you used to find the lengths of the rectangles.

DO MORE

Write an equation showing the relationship between the length and width of the rectangular pen that has a perimeter of 24 yd.   L = _____

Name _____ Date _____

Perimeter Puzzle

Materials: uncooked spaghetti noodles, ruler

Mr. Jones wants to build a rectangular pen for his dog. He has space for a pen with a width of 5 yards. Fencing comes in 1-yard sections.

1. If Mr. Jones decides to buy 22 yards of fencing, what will be the length of his dog's pen? Follow the directions below to find out.

   a. Cut an uncooked spaghetti noodle to a length of 22 cm. Each centimeter of the noodle will represent a 1-yard section of fencing.

   b. Cut off two 5-cm pieces off the noodle to form the sides of the rectangle. How long is the piece of noodle you have left?

   c. How would you cut the remaining piece of noodle to create the top and bottom of the rectangle?

   d. What is the length of this rectangle?

   W = 5 cm   L = _____ cm

2. The perimeter, P of a rectangle is the total distance around. Find the length of the pen if Mr. Jones decides to buy each of the following amounts of fencing. Cut uncooked spaghetti noodles to the correct lengths to model the different fencing options. Use these models to help you find the correct lengths.

W	5	5	5	5
P	22	20	18	16
L				

0-7424-2884-2 *Using the Standards—Algebra*

Name _____ Date _____

Perimeter Puzzle (cont.)

3. Explain the process you used to find the lengths.

4. Write an equation showing how to find the length of the pen for any perimeter, P, when the width of the pen is 5 yards.

L = _____

5. Mr. Jones decided to put the pen in a different spot. He decides to experiment with different widths and perimeters. Find the length of each pen. Cut uncooked spaghetti noodles to the correct lengths to model the different fencing options. Use these models to help you find the correct lengths.

W	5	6	7	8
P	20	24	22	26
L				

6. Explain how to find the length of a rectangle if you know the perimeter and the width.

DO MORE

Write an equation showing how to find the length of the pen for any perimeter, P, and any width, W.   L = _____

0-7424-2884-2 *Using the Standards—Algebra*

Name _____ Date _____

To the Max

Materials: uncooked spaghetti noodles, ruler

Mr. Jones just bought 20 yards of fencing to make a pen for his dog. He will make the pen in the shape of a rectangle. The fencing comes in 1-yard sections. He wants as big a space as possible for his dog to run around. What dimensions will give a pen with the maximum area?

1. Use uncooked spaghetti noodles to model this situation. The noodles will model the fencing, with each 1 centimeter representing 1 yard of fencing. Cut several strands of noodles into pieces that are 20 cm long. Discard remaining noodle parts.

2. Make a table showing the length of each rectangular pen with the following widths.

width (cm)	1	2	3	4	5	6	7	8	9
length (cm)									

3. Explain how you found your answers to problem 2.

4. Use uncooked spaghetti noodles to create each different rectangle. Which one do you think will have the greatest area? Why?

0-7424-2884-2 *Using the Standards—Algebra*

To the Max (cont.)

The area of a rectangle can be found by multiplying the length by the width.

---

5. Copy your answers from question 3 into this table. Then find the area of each rectangle and add it to the table.

width (cm)	1	2	3	4	5	6	7	8	9
length (cm)									
area (sq. cm)									

6. Which dimensions gave the largest area? _____

7. What dimensions should Mr. Jones use to get the maximum area if he buys 32 yards of fencing? Make a table of widths, lengths, and areas. Circle the dimensions with the largest area.

width (cm)								
length (cm)								
area (sq. cm)								

8. What dimensions should Mr. Jones use to get the maximum area if he buys 28 yards of fencing? Make a table of widths, lengths, and areas. Circle the dimensions with the largest area.

width (cm)								
length (cm)								
area (sq. cm)								

THINK

What do you notice about the rectangles with the largest areas?

0-7424-2884-2 *Using the Standards—Algebra*

Name _____ Date _____

Create Your Own Problems

1. Pick two different types of objects (jellybeans, pennies, popcorn kernels, marbles, etc.). Use a scale to see how many of each type of object is needed to balance the scale. Write some questions about how the weights of the objects compare. See if a friend can find the correct balance between the objects and answer the questions.

2. Choose two differently-sized boxes (like a shoe box and a cereal box). Take some measurements and write some questions about the volume of the boxes. See if a friend can answer your questions.

3. Write some questions about rectangles.

   a. Give the perimeter and the width and ask someone to find the length.

   b. Give the perimeter and the width and ask someone to find the length and the area.

   c. Have someone experiment with different widths and perimeters to see how this affects the length and the area.

0-7424-2884-2 *Using the Standards—Algebra*

Name _____ Date _____

Check Your Skills

1. Two pennies weigh the same amount as 1 quarter.

    a. Write an equation to show the relationship if *P* is the weight of a penny and *Q* is the weight of a quarter.

    b. How many pennies would it take to balance 11 quarters? Show your work.

    c. How many quarters would it take to balance 30 pennies? Show your work.

2. A rectangular prism has a base with a width of 3 cm, a length of 2 cm, and a height of 7 cm.

    a. Use centimeter cubes to build a model of this prism.

    b. How many cubes make up the base area of the prism? _____

    c. How many layers of cubes are there? _____

    d. What is the volume of the prism? _____

    e. Write an equation that shows the relationship between the volume (V), the width (W), the length (L), and the height (H) of the prism. _____

3. A rectangle has a perimeter of 16 cm.

    a. Write an equation showing the relationship between the width (W) and the length (L) of the rectangle. _____

    b. What dimensions of the rectangle will give it the largest possible area? Show your work.

     0-7424-2884-2 *Using the Standards—Algebra*

Name _____ Date _____

Stretched to the Limit

Materials: rubber bands, paperclips, paper cups, pennies, ruler

Many objects, such as ropes, cables, and bungee chords have elasticity. This is what helps them to stretch rather than break when weight or tension is placed on them. In this activity, you will use rubber bands to model how various factors affect an object's elasticity.

Find the relationship between weight and the amount of stretch in the rubber band.

1.   What do you think will happen to the rubber band if you add more and more weight to the cup? Make a prediction.

Loop a couple of rubber bands together. Poke holes near the top on either side of a small paper cup. Unbend a paperclip. Loop it through the bottom of one of the rubber bands, and use it to hold the paper cup.

2.   Loop the top rubber band over your finger or a pencil so it is hanging down with the cup attached to it. Measure the length of the rubber band.   L = _____

3.   Use pennies as weights. Add pennies to the cup, one at a time. After adding each penny, measure the length of the rubber band. Record your answers in the table below.

weight (# of pennies)	length

0-7424-2884-2 *Using the Standards—Algebra*

Name _____ Date _____

Stretched to the Limit (cont.)

4. Make a coordinate graph of your data. Choose a scale. Plot the points.

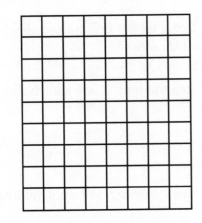

Length

Weight (# of pennies)

5. Write a sentence to describe the relationship between the length the rubber band stretches and the weight attached.

6. Use your graph and table to make predictions about stretch lengths for weights that you have not yet tested. Then test your predictions.

THINK

Did you get the same results as others in your class? Did your rubber bands stretch the same amounts as a classmate's? Why or why not?

Published by Instructional Fair. Copyright protected.

0-7424-2884-2 *Using the Standards—Algebra*

Name _____ Date _____

Up and Down

Materials: a ball, watch with second hand or stop watch, meter sticks

Toss a ball straight up in to the air and let it hit the floor. Don't let the ball hit a ceiling if you are inside. Practice this a few times. Watch how the ball moves.

1. Describe what happened to the height of the ball from the time it left your hand until it reached the floor. Be specific.

2. Describe what happened to the speed of the ball from the time it left your hand until it reached the floor. Be specific.

3. Which of the following graphs most accurately shows the relationship between the time the ball was in the air and the height the ball was from the ground? Explain your reasoning.

a.

Height Above Ground (inches) / Time (seconds)

b.

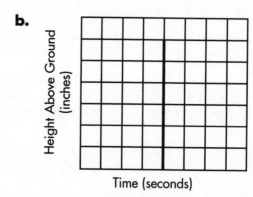

Height Above Ground (inches) / Time (seconds)

c.

Height Above Ground (inches) / Time (seconds)

d.

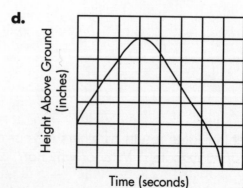

Height Above Ground (inches) / Time (seconds)

0-7424-2884-2 *Using the Standards—Algebra*

Up and Down (cont.)

Take some measurements. Get some help from your classmates. Decide where you are going to release the ball. Measure that height from the ground in centimeters using a meter stick. Tack a long strip of paper up on the wall, next to where you will throw the ball. You will throw the ball straight up next to the wall. Make sure the ball does not hit the wall, ceiling, or any other object on its way back down.

Have a friend time how long the ball is in the air. Begin timing as soon as the ball leaves your hands and stop as soon as it touches the floor. Also, note at what time the ball hits its highest point. Another friend should watch to see how high the ball goes and mark that point on the strip of paper. Finally, use the marking on the paper to measure how high the ball went.

4. How long was the ball in the air? _____

5. How high was the ball at its starting point? _____

6. What was the maximum height of the ball in the air? _____

7. Make a coordinate graph that shows the relationship between the time the ball is in the air and the height of the ball from the ground. Use the measurements you found to help you make the coordinate graph.

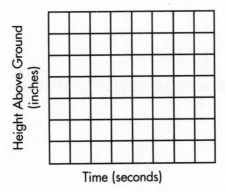

DO MORE

Describe the relationship between time and height in your graph. Be specific and include exact measurements.

0-7424-2884-2 *Using the Standards—Algebra*

Name _____ Date _____

FAN-tastic!

A city just acquired a new ice-hockey team called the Slushies. Each month, the Slushies gained more fans, as shown in the following table.

number of months	1	2	3	4	5	6
number of fans	100	200	400			

1. Make a coordinate graph showing the relationship between the number of months and the number of fans.

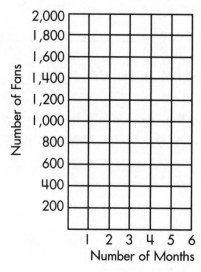

2. Describe the graph.

0-7424-2884-2 *Using the Standards—Algebra*

Name _____ Date _____

FAN-tastic! (cont.)

3. What happens to the number of fans each month?

4. If this pattern continues, how many fans will the Slushies have after 6 months?
Show your work.

5. If this pattern continues, how long will it take before the Slushies have over 25,000 fans?
Explain how you found your answer.

6. If this pattern continues, how many fans will the Slushies have after 12 months?
Show your work.

THINK

Do you think it is reasonable to believe this pattern will continue indefinitely? Explain.

Name _____ Date _____

Making Money

Kanisha's dad has his own business. Over summer vacation, Kanisha is earning money by working for her dad. She helps by doing odd jobs around the office, such as filing papers and answering the phone. Her dad is paying her $5.00 an hour.

1. How much will Kanisha make in a week if she works 2 hours? _____

How much will she earn in 3 hours? _____

2. Fill in the table to show how much money Kanisha will make in a week if she works the given number of hours.

# of hours	0	1	2	3	4	5	6
amt. earned							

3. Make a coordinate graph to show the relationship between the number of hours Kanisha works and how much money she earns.

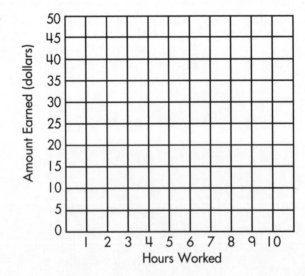

0-7424-2884-2 *Using the Standards—Algebra*

Name _____ Date _____

Making Money (cont.)

4. Use words to describe the relationship between the number of hours Kanisha works and the amount of money she makes. How is this shown in the table? How is this shown in the graph?

5. How much money will Kanisha make in a week if she works $5\frac{1}{2}$ hours? Show how you got your answer.

6. If Kanisha made $45, how many hours did she work that week? Show how you got your answer.

7. Write an equation showing a relationship between the number of hours Kanisha works, *H*, and the amount of money she earns that week, *A*.

8. If Kanisha works 40 hours in 1 month, how much will she have earned? Explain how you can use the equation you wrote in question 7 to get your answer.

DO MORE

After a month, Kanisha's dad offers to give her $6 an hour because she is doing such a great job. Make a table and coordinate graph showing how much money she will make working from 1 to 10 hours. Write an equation showing the relationship. How do the table, graph, and equation compare to those made when she was making $5 an hour?

0-7424-2884-2 *Using the Standards—Algebra*

Name _____ Date _____

Ferris Wheel

Takoda and Dylan are riding on a Ferris Wheel at the county fair. The ride lasts for 3 minutes before they begin loading and unloading passengers for the next ride. The graph below shows the boys' height above the ground during the 3-minute ride. Use the graph to answer the questions.

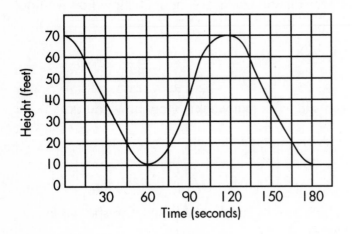

1. Where on the Ferris Wheel were the boys sitting when the ride started? Explain how this is shown on the graph.

2. How high is the bottom of the Ferris Wheel from the ground? Explain how this is shown on the graph.

Published by Instructional Fair. Copyright protected.

0-7424-2884-2 *Using the Standards—Algebra*

Ferris Wheel (cont.)

3. How high is the center of the Ferris Wheel from the ground? Explain how this is shown on the graph.

4. How much time does the Ferris Wheel take to make one complete revolution? Explain how this is shown on the graph.

5. Where on the Ferris Wheel were the boys sitting when the ride ended? Explain how this is shown on the graph.

6. Does the graph show the actual path that the Ferris Wheel took? Explain.

7. How high were the boys from the ground halfway through the ride? Explain how this is shown on the graph.

8. How many revolutions did the boys make during their ride? Explain how this is shown on the graph.

THINK

How would the graph look if the same Ferris Wheel rotated twice as fast?

95

Name _____ Date _____

Cube Curiosity

Materials: cubes

A variable changes at a **constant rate** if it increases or decreases by the same amount every time.

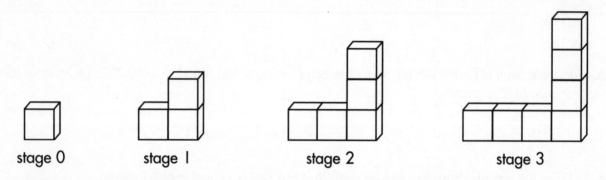

stage 0   stage 1   stage 2   stage 3

1. Use cubes to build models like those pictured above. Find the volume (number of cubes) of each model. Find the pattern and build the next 3 models in the pattern. Complete the table below.

stage	0	1	2	3	4	5	6
volume	1						

2. What happens to the volume of the models as the stage increases? Does the volume change at a constant rate? How can you tell by looking at the table?

3. What would be the volume of a model at stage 10? Show how you got your answer.

4. Use another piece of paper to make a coordinate graph showing the relationship between the stage and the number of cubes.

0-7424-2884-2 *Using the Standards—Algebra*

Name _____ Date _____

Cube Curiosity (cont.)

5. Write an equation showing the relationship between the volume, V, and the stage, S. Test your equation by plugging in numbers from your table.

V = _____

Now look at the surface area of the models. The surface area is the number of squares on the outside of the model. At stage 0 there is only 1 cube. A cube has 6 square sides, so its surface area is 6 square units. At stage 1, there are 14 square units of surface area.

6. Build each model and find its surface area. Record your answers in the table below. Do not forget to count the area on the bottom of the model.

stage	0	1	2	3	4	5	6
surface area	6	14					

7. What happens to the surface area of the models as the stage increases? Does the surface area change at a constant rate? How can you tell by looking at the table?

8. What would be the surface area of a model at stage 10? Show how you got your answer.

9. Use another piece of paper to make a coordinate graph showing the relationship between the stage and the surface area.

10. Write an equation showing the relationship between the surface area, A, and the stage, S. Test your equation by plugging in numbers from your table.

A = _____

THINK

Compare the graphs you made of volume and surface area. How do these graphs look similar? What do the graphs tell you about the rates of change between the variables?

97

Name _____   Date _____

Building Pyramids

Materials: cubes

A variable changes at a **constant rate** if it increases or decreases by the same amount every time. If it changes by different amounts each time, then it changes at a **varying rate**.

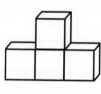
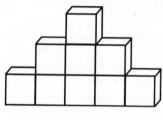

stage 0   stage 1   stage 2

1.   Use cubes to build models like those pictured above. Find the volume (number of cubes) of each model. Find the pattern and build the next 3 models in the pattern. Complete the table below.

stage	0	1	2	3	4	5	6
volume	1						

2.   What happens to the volume of the models as the stage increases? Does the volume change at a constant rate? How can you tell by looking at the table?

Building Pyramids (cont.)

3. Describe the pattern of change in the volume of cubes.

4. What would be the volume of a model at stage 8? Show how you got your answer.

5. Make a coordinate graph showing the relationship between the stage and the number of cubes.

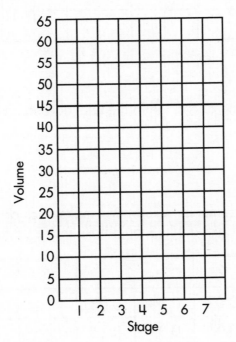

THINK

How can you tell the type of change (constant or varying) by looking at the graph?

0-7424-2884-2 *Using the Standards—Algebra*

Name _____ Date _____

Dollars and Sense

Jeremy's mother offers to pay him to do some extra chores around the house. She says she will pay him $2 a day. Jeremy says he wants only 1 penny the first day, 2 pennies the second day, 4 pennies the third day, 8 pennies the fourth day, and so on. Should his mother accept his offer?

1. Which plan do you think is better for Jeremy? Which plan is better for his mother? Why?

2. Make a table showing how much money Jeremy will make over the first 15 days if he takes his mother's offer.

# of days	1	2	3	4	5	6	7	8	9	10	11	12	13	14	15
total $ earned	2	4	6												

3. Is there a constant or varying rate of change in the total earned under Jeremy's mother's plan? Explain.

4. Make a table showing how much money Jeremy will make *each* day if his mother accepts his offer. Then calculate the total amount he would have made up to that point.

# of days	1	2	3	4	5	6	7	8
$ amt. earned	0.01	0.02	0.04	0.08				
total $ earned	0.01	0.03	0.07	0.15				

# of days	9	10	11	12	13	14	15	16
$ amt. earned								
total $ earned								

0-7424-2884-2 *Using the Standards—Algebra*

Name _____ Date _____

Dollars and Sense (cont.)

5. Is there a constant or varying rate of change in the total earned under Jeremy's mother's plan? Explain.

6. Compare the tables. Which plan would be better for Jeremy if he only worked 10 days? Explain.

7. If Jeremy works 15 days, which plan would be better for him? Explain.

8. Under what conditions would it be best for Jeremy to accept his mother's offer? Explain.

9. Under what conditions would it be best for Jeremy to use his own plan? Explain.

THINK

Did the results of the two plans turn out the way you thought they would?

0-7424-2884-2 *Using the Standards—Algebra*

Name _____ Date _____

Speeding Spectacular

A variable changes at a **constant rate** if it increases or decreases by the same amount every time. If it changes by different amounts each time, then it changes at a **varying rate**.

The Montgomery family traveled 400 miles to a campground for their vacation.

1. Write an equation showing the relationship between the amount of time, _T_, they spent driving and the average speed, _S_, that the car traveled. _____

2. Find the average speed they would have had to drive to make the trip in the given number of hours. Fill in the table. Round the speed values to the nearest ones digit.

Time (hours)	4	5	6	7	8	9	10
Speed (miles/hour)							

3. Describe the relationship between the time of the trip and the average speed.

4. Graph the relationship between time and speed on another piece of paper.

5. Does the average speed change at a constant rate or a varying rate? Explain how you can tell by looking at the table and the graph.

THINK

How can you look at a graph to determine if a variable changes at a constant rate?

0-7424-2884-2 _Using the Standards—Algebra_

Name _____   Date _____

Go Gravity!

A variable changes at a **constant rate** if it increases or decreases by the same amount every time. If it changes by different amounts each time, then it changes at a **varying rate**.

A penny is dropped from the top of a 100-meter building. The following graph shows the height of the penny from the ground at any particular time. Use the graph to answer the questions.

1. Describe the relationship between the height of the penny above the ground and the time.

2. Does the height change at a constant rate or a varying rate? How do you know?

3. How long did it take the penny to hit the ground? Explain how you found your answer.

4. How far above the ground was the penny after 2 seconds? Explain how you found your answer.

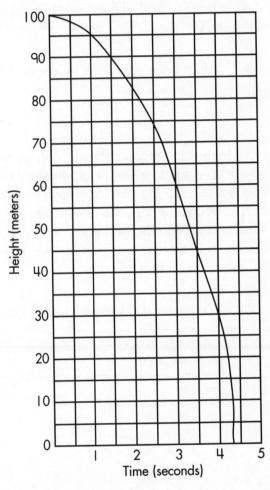

THINK

What happened to the speed of the penny as it fell? Did it stay the same, slow down, or get faster? How can you tell this by looking at the graph?

0-7424-2884-2 *Using the Standards—Algebra*

Name _____ Date _____

Give It Some Bounce

A variable changes at a **constant rate** if it increases or decreases by the same amount every time. If it changes by different amounts each time, then it changes at a **varying rate**.

Materials: a bouncy ball, meter sticks, paper, pencil

Hold a bouncy ball above your head. Drop the ball on a hard floor. Watch what happens as it bounces.

1. What happens to the height of the ball at each bounce?

Now take some measurements. Get some help from some of your classmates. Tack a long strip of paper up against a wall. Hold the ball up above your head. Mark the place on the paper where you will release the ball. Someone should watch carefully to see how high the ball would go after its first bounce. Mark that spot on the paper. Then drop the ball again from the starting height. Watch how high the ball goes on the second bounce. If the ball hits any object besides the floor during its bouncing, you will have to repeat this again. Continue to do this until you get as many heights marked as you can.

2. Use meter sticks to measure the heights and record them in the table below.

# of bounces	0	1	2	3	4	5	6
height							

0-7424-2884-2 *Using the Standards—Algebra*

Name _____ Date _____

Give It Some Bounce (cont.)

3. Make a coordinate graph that shows the relationship between the number of bounces and the height of the ball.

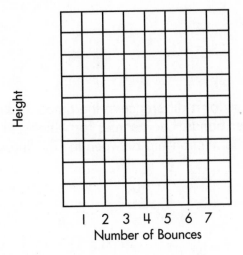

4. Does the height of the ball decrease by the same amount at each bounce? Explain how you can use the table and the graph to get your answer.

5. Does the height of the ball change at a constant rate or a varying rate? Explain.

THINK

What would happen if you used a different type of ball? Would the pattern between the height and number of bounces be similar?

0-7424-2884-2 *Using the Standards—Algebra*

Create Your Own Problems

I. Use cubes to make models. Create a pattern using your cubes. Ask questions about your model pattern. You might ask about surface area or volume.

2. Design an experiment that tests for a difference in the amount of stretch between thin rubber bands and thick rubber bands. Use pennies for weights to make the rubber bands stretch. Ask questions about the relationship between the thickness and the amount of stretch.

3. Write a problem that relates distance, speed, and time. Ask a classmate to write an equation, make a table, and make a coordinate graph. Ask whether there is a constant or varying rate of change.

4. Sketch four different graphs. Ask a classmate to decide which graph(s) show a constant rate of change and which graphs show a varying rate of change.

0-7424-2884-2 *Using the Standards—Algebra*

Name _____ Date _____

Check Your Skills

1. An elastic bungee chord used as a tie-down has a length of 24 inches when it is hanging straight down. Weights are hooked to the bottom of the chord to make it stretch. The following table shows the measurements taken.

weight (lbs.)	0	1	2	3	4	5	6	7	8
length (in.)	24	26	28	30	32	34	36	38	40

a. Does the length increase at a constant rate or at a varying rate? Explain.

b. Write an equation showing the relationship between the weight, W, and the length, L.

c. If the bungee chord had 12 pounds on the end, how far would it stretch? Show your work.

2. Brooke is babysitting her little brother. Her dad agreed to pay her $3 an hour.

a. How much will Brooke make if she watches him for 3 hours? 5 hours?

b. Over the weekend, Brooke made $27. How many hours did she work?

c. Write an equation showing the relationship between the hours, H, she works and the amount of money, M, that she earns.

0-7424-2884-2 *Using the Standards—Algebra*

Name _____ Date _____

Check Your Skills (cont.)

3. A particular rubber ball bounces half its height each consecutive bounce. It started at a height of 72 inches.

a. Make a table of the ball's height for the first 4 bounces.

b. Make a coordinate graph showing the relationship between the number of bounces and the ball's height above the ground.

c. Does the height of the ball decrease at a constant rate or at a varying rate? Explain.

4. Look at each of the graphs. Which graphs show a constant rate of change and which show a varying rate of change?

a.

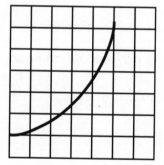

b.

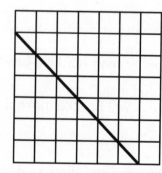

c.

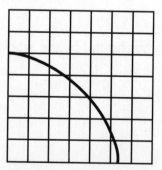

d.

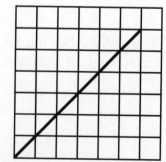

0-7424-2884-2 *Using the Standards—Algebra*

Posttest

1. Find the next three numbers in each pattern. Describe each of the following patterns. Circle the one(s) that grow at a constant rate.

   a. 8   9   11   14   18   23   _____ _____ _____ _____
   b. 12   17   22   27   32   37   _____ _____ _____ _____
   c. 6   9   15   24   39   63   _____ _____ _____ _____

2. A function machine uses a rule to change numbers. Look for a pattern between the IN and OUT numbers in the table. Fill in the missing numbers. Write the rule.

IN	10	6		22	18	44
OUT	22		27	34		56

   Rule: _____

3. What property (commutative, associative, or distributive) was used to rewrite each equation?

   a. $5 + (3 + 2) = 5 + (2 + 3)$ _____
   b. $4 \times (8 + 7) = 4 \times 8 + 4 \times 7$ _____
   c. $(31 + 20) + 11 = 31 + (20 + 11)$ _____

4. Each symbol stands for a number. Find the numbers that make both equations true.

   a.   🌼 + 🕷 = 15

        🕷 ÷ 🌼 = 2

        🌼 = _____

        🕷 = _____

   b.   ♡ × ◇ = 40

        ♡ − ◇ = 18

        ♡ = _____

        ◇ = _____

5. Alisha and Samantha are selling cotton candy at the school carnival. Alisha sells 9 more bags than Samantha. Alisha sold A bags and Samantha sold S bags.

   a. Write an equation showing this relationship.
   b. If Alisha sold 52 bags, how many did Samantha sell?
   c. If Samantha sold 34 bags, how many did Alisha sell?

0-7424-2884-2 *Using the Standards—Algebra*

Posttest (cont.)

6. A farmer has 52 yards of fencing to put around his rectangular cow pasture. The fencing comes in 1-yard sections.

    a. Make a table showing all the different dimensions his pasture could have.

    b. What dimensions will give him the largest possible area? Show your work.

7. Tiles were arranged in a pattern as shown. Use squares or tiles to make the patterns. Build the next three models in the pattern.

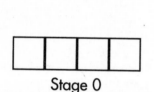

Stage 0

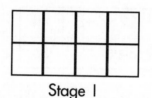

Stage 1

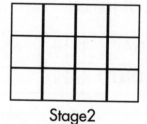

Stage2

    a. Make a table showing the relationship between the stage and the area of each model.

Stage	0	1	2	3	4	5
Area						

    b. Write an equation showing the relationship between the stage, S, and the area, A.

    c. Does the area increase at a constant rate or a varying rate? How do you know?

8. Bryan earns $2 an hour raking leaves.

    a. Fill in the table showing the relationship between the number of hours he works and the amount he earns.

Hours	1	2	3	4	5	6	7	8
Amount (in $)								

    b. Write an equation showing the relationship between hours worked, *H*, and amount earned, *A*.

    c. If Bryan works 15 hours, how much will he make? Show your work.

0-7424-2884-2 *Using the Standards—Algebra*

Answer Key

Pretest . . . .**pages 7–8**

1. a. repeating; ABBABB

   b. growing; × 3

   c. decreasing; − 66

2. OUT = IN ÷ 9

IN	27	9	81	36	54	45
OUT	3	1	9	4	6	5

3. a. $V = 409$

   b. $T = 1{,}344$

   c. $W = 4$

   d. $S = 642$

4. $S = 10, C = 5, T = 7, V = 8$

5. a. $300 = 50 \times T$

   b. 6 hours

6. a. $B = 3 \times M$

   b. 9 marbles

   c. 6 blocks

7. Graph D

8. a. $D = 60 \times T$

   b.

Time	1	2	3	4	5	6	7
Distance	60	120	180	240	300	360	420

   c.

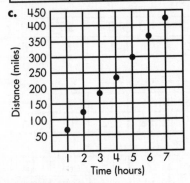

   d. constant rate

Doing the Bunny Hop . . . .**page 9**

1. a. Stick your foot out twice, hop twice, and repeat.

   b. AABB

2. a. Hop twice, kneel down on all four legs, then repeat.

   b. AAB

3. a. Stand on all fours, hop, and then stick out a foot. Repeat.

   b. ABC

Polygon Patterns . . . .**page 10**

1. hexagon, triangle, hexagon, triangle, hexagon, triangle; ABAB

2. pentagon, pentagon, square, pentagon, pentagon, square; AAB

3. octagon, octagon, trapezoid, trapezoid, octagon, octagon, trapezoid, trapezoid; AABB

4. pentagon, rectangle, rectangle, rectangle, pentagon, rectangle, rectangle, rectangle, pentagon; ABBB

Shape Patterns . . . .**page 11**

1. parallelogram, trapezoid, trapezoid, parallelogram, trapezoid, trapezoid, parallelogram; ABB

2. kite, square, square, kite, square, square, kite, square, square; ABB

3. trapezoid, rhombus, rhombus, trapezoid, rhombus, rhombus, trapezoid, rhombus; ABB

4. All three have the same type of pattern.

Number Parade . . . .**page 12**

1. 5 9 4 5 9 4 5 9 4; ABC

2. 3 3 6 3 3 6 3 3 6; AAB

3. 1 1 2 2 1 1 2 2 1 1; AABB

4. 1 5 5 7 1 5 5 7 1 5 5 7; ABBC

5. 2 2 8 2 2 8 2 2 8; AAB

6. 4 7 1 4 7 1 4 7 1; ABC

Percussion Patterns . . . .**page 13**

Observe each group's rhythm to make sure it matches the patterns.

Pattern Match-Up . . . .**page 14**

1. C

2. D

3. A

4. B

Delightful Designs . . . .**page 15**

1. a. The shading alternates from the empty triangles to the triangles containing shapes.

   b. The shapes rotate between every other triangle in a clockwise direction.

   c.

2.

   a. 6 dots

   b. 5 segments

To Grow or Not to Grow . . . .**page 16**

1. 59, 70, 81; growing; Add 11 each time.

2. 554, 455, 356; decreasing; Subtract 99 each time.

3. 45, 24, 3; decreasing; Subtract 21 each time.

4. 412, 493, 574; growing; Add 81 each time.

0-7424-2884-2 *Using the Standards—Algebra*

Answer Key

Going Up or Coming Down? . . . . .page 17

1. 72, 24, 8; decreasing; Divide by 3 each time.
2. 648; 1,944; 5,832; increasing; Multiply by 3 each time.
3. 48, 96, 192; increasing; Multiply by 2 each time.
4. 12, 6, 3; decreasing; Divide by 2 each time.

The Case of the Missing Numbers . . . . .page 18

1. 3, 8, 13, 18, 23, 28, 33, 38; + 5
2. 50,000,000; 5,000,000; 500,000; 50,000; 5,000; 500; 50; ÷ 10
3. 722, 656, 590, 524, 458, 392, 326, 260; – 66
4. 1.25; 5; 20; 80; 320; 1,280; 5,120; 20,480; × 4

Rule of Thumb . . . . .page 19

1. 7, 14, 28, 56, 112, 224, 448, 896
2. 896, 448, 224, 112, 56, 28, 14, 7
3. 830, 719, 608, 497, 386, 275, 164, 53
4. 53, 164, 275, 386, 497, 608, 719, 830

Fill in the Blanks .page 20

1. 15, 37, 59, 81, 103, 125, 147, 169; + 22
2. 58, 50, 42, 34, 26, 18, 10, 2; – 8
3. 8, 30, 52, 74, 96, 118, 140, 162; + 22
4. 63, 55, 47, 39, 31, 23, 15, 7; – 8

Keeping It Steady . . . . .pages 21–22

1. a. growing
   b. No. The amount of change is always different (+ 1, + 2, + 3…).
   c. The amount of change increases by 1 more each time (+ 1 + 2 + 3 + 4 + 5…).
   d. 40, 49, 59
2. a. decreasing
   b. Yes. The amount of change is always 3.
   c. To find the next number, subtract 3 from the previous number.
   d. 8, 5, 2
3. a. decreasing
   b. No. The amount of change is always different (– 18, – 16, – 14…).
   c. The amount of change decreases by the next smaller even consecutive integer.
   d. 235, 229, 225
4. a. growing
   b. No. The amount of change is always different (+ 1, + 3, + 5…).
   c. The amount of change increases by the next consecutive odd integer.
   d. 255, 268, 283

A Tidy Sum . . . . .page 23

1. a. growing
   b. No. The amount of change is always different.
   c. Add the previous two numbers in the pattern.
   d. 97, 157, 254
2. a. decreasing
   b. No. The amount of change is always different.
   c. Subtract the previous two numbers in the pattern.
   d. 9, 6, 3

Function Machine .page 24

1. OUT: 27, 20, 23, 22, 25
2. OUT: 15, 1, 30, 24
3. OUT: 48, 32, 8, 80, 24

Follow the Rules .page 25

1.
IN	2	3	6	8	11	14
OUT	9	10	13	15	18	21

2.
IN	25	12	35	103	56	81
OUT	13	0	23	91	44	69

3.
IN	15	8	4	21	3	9
OUT	60	32	16	84	12	36

4.
IN	12	48	84	36	90	30
OUT	2	8	14	6	15	5

In and Out . . . . .page 26

1.
IN	3	9	11	6	8
OUT	6	18	22	12	16

Rule: OUT = IN x 2

2.
IN	4	7	19	44	18
OUT	12	15	27	52	26

Rule: OUT = IN + 8

3.
IN	55	38	72	61	80
OUT	26	9	43	32	51

Rule: OUT = IN – 29

4.
IN	108	27	63	126	18
OUT	12	3	7	14	2

Rule: OUT = IN ÷ 9

Function Junction . . . . .page 27

1.
IN	41	28	110	37	55	86
OUT	26	13	95	22	40	71

Rule: OUT = IN – 15

0-7424-2884-2 *Using the Standards—Algebra*

Answer Key

2.

IN	4	8	9	14	5	25
OUT	24	48	54	84	30	150

Rule: OUT = IN x 6

3.

IN	32	9	22	65	48	13
OUT	39	16	29	72	55	20

Rule: OUT = IN + 7

4.

IN	21	28	35	63	91	56
OUT	3	4	5	9	13	8

Rule: OUT = IN ÷ 7

In a Word . . . . **pages 28–29**

1. IN: number of stickers Sharon has

OUT: number of stickers Grace has

Rule: OUT = IN + 12

IN	0	5	6	11
OUT	12	17	18	23

2. IN: number of strawberries Joe ate

OUT: number of strawberries Miguel ate

Rule: OUT = IN − 3

IN	15	18	22	25
OUT	12	15	19	22

3. IN: number of trading cards Deshawn has

OUT: number of trading cards Darnell has

Rule: OUT = IN x 2

IN	3	7	12	15
OUT	6	14	24	30

4. IN: number of cartoons Chu drew

OUT: number of cartoons Lashanda drew

Rule: OUT = IN + 4

IN	5	18	12	15
OUT	9	22	16	19

5. IN: number of words Chad got correct

OUT: number of words Kendra got correct

Rule: OUT = IN − 4

IN	17	18	20	31
OUT	13	14	16	27

6. IN: number of bracelets Anna has

OUT: number of bracelets Chantelle has

Rule: OUT = IN x 3

IN	2	4	9	12
OUT	6	12	27	36

Snow Day . . . . **pages 30–31**

1. 2 x $3 = $6; 5 x $3 = $15; 7 x $3 = $21

2. Money earned = 10 entries x $3

3. Money earned = N x $3

4.

# of entries	2	5	7	8	10	14
money earned	6	15	21	24	30	42

5.

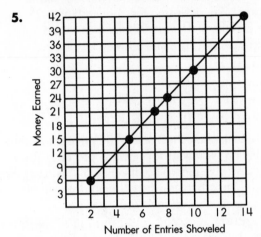

6. Each time another entryway is shoveled, the money earned goes up $3.

Check Your Skills . . . . **page 33**

1. a. 51, 60, 69; growing; + 9

b. 7, 2, 7; repeating; AAB

c. 74, 48, 22; decreasing; − 26

2. a. 39, 63, 102; add the previous 2 numbers

b. 27, 31, 35; add 4 each time; grows at a constant rate

3.

IN	3	5	6	9	10	12
OUT	24	40	48	72	80	96

Rule: x 8

Marble Mayhem . . . . **page 34**

1. 34; 14 + 20 = 34

2. 34; 20 + 14 = 34

3. 34; no

4. addition; no

5. a. 25; 25

b. 112; 112

c. 412; 412

d. 1,280; 1,280

Pinching Pennies . . . . **page 35**

1. 12; 3 x 4 = 12

2. 12; 4 x 3 = 12

3. 12; no

4. multiplication; no

5. a. 108; 108

b. 2,592; 2,592

c. 2,366; 2,366

d. 1,131; 1,131

6. Products will vary. No.

Published by Instructional Fair. Copyright protected.

0-7424-2884-2 *Using the Standards—Algebra*

Answer Key

Groovy Groupings . . . . .page 36

1. $7 + (14 + 22) = 7 + 36 = 43$

2. They grouped the numbers differently. Juanita found the sum of 7 and 14 and then added that to 22. Emily found the sum of 14 and 22 and then added that to 7. They both got the same answer.

3. **a.** 125; 125
   b. 183; $126 + (18 + 39) = 183$
   c. 499; $44 + (25 + 430) = 499$
   d. 934; $(256 + 110) + 568 = 934$

4. Yes. Students should test several different combinations of changing groupings for addition problems. They should also give reasoning of why it makes sense that changing the grouping when adding does not change the answer.

Principled Products . . . . .page 37

1. $(8 \times 4) \times 6 = 32 \times 6 = 192$

2. They grouped the numbers differently. Yes.

3. **a.** 90; $(3 \times 15) \times 2 = 90$
   b. 540; $6 \times (10 \times 9) = 540$
   c. 60; $4 \times (5 \times 3) = 60$
   d. 2,200; $(25 \times 11) \times 8 = 2,200$

4. Yes. Students should test several different combinations of changing groupings for multiplication problems. They should also give reasoning of why it makes sense that changing the grouping when adding does not change the answer.

Which Property? . . . . .page 38

1. $15 + (87 + 12) = 114$; $(15 + 87) + 12 = 102 + 12 = 114$; associative

2. $27 \times 61 = 1,647$; $61 \times 27 = 1,647$; commutative

3. $(3 \times 16) \times 2 = 48 \times 2 = 96$; $3 \times (16 \times 2) = 3 \times 32 = 96$; associative

4. $12 + (82 + 65) = 12 + 147 = 159$; $12 + (65 + 82) = 12 + 147 = 159$; commutative

5. $312 + 77 = 389$; $77 + 312 = 389$; commutative

6. $75 + (18 + 39) = 75 + 57 = 132$; $(75 + 18) + 39 = 93 + 39 = 132$; associative

Puzzling Properties .page 39

1. 1,131; $87 \times 13 = 1,131$

2. 240; $57 + 183 = 240$

3. 1,817; $23 \times 79 = 1,817$

4. 395; $(45 + 38) + 312 = 395$ OR $312 + (38 + 45) = 395$

5. 189; $22 + (76 + 91) = 189$

6. 210; $(3 \times 14) \times 5 = 210$

7. 168; $12 \times (7 \times 2) = 168$

Making Models . . . . .pages 40–41

1. 3×4

2. 12

3. 3×5

4. 15

5. 27

6. $3 \times 4 + 3 \times 5 = 12 + 15 = 27$; yes

7. The models are the same, but Janelle has pushed the grid of white squares and the grid of shaded squares together.

8. The total number of columns of white and shaded squares combined.

9. There are 3 rows of 9 columns, so multiplying 3 by 9 will find the total number of squares.

10. Yes. The models are the same. The number of squares did not change. There is just two different equations that represent the model.

Model This . . . . .page 42

Check students' drawn models.

1. $5 \times 8 + 5 \times 3 = 5 \times (8 + 3)$; $40 + 15 = 5 \times 11$; $55 = 55$

2. $7 \times (2 + 5) = 7 \times 2 + 7 \times 5$; $7 \times 7 = 14 + 35$; $49 = 49$

3. $6 \times 4 + 6 \times 3 = 6 \times (4 + 3)$; $24 + 18 = 6 \times 7$; $42 = 42$

Break Down . . . . .page 43

1. $76 \times 3 = (70 + 6) \times 3 = 70 \times 3 + 6 \times 3 = 210 + 18 = 228$

2. $84 \times 6 = (80 + 4) \times 6 = 80 \times 6 + 4 \times 6 = 480 + 24 = 504$

3. $45 \times 7 = (40 + 5) \times 7 = 40 \times 7 + 5 \times 7 = 280 + 35 = 315$

4. $98 \times 2 = (90 + 8) \times 2 = 90 \times 2 + 8 \times 2 = 180 + 16 = 196$

5. $29 \times 8 = (20 + 9) \times 8 = 20 \times 8 + 9 \times 8 = 160 + 72 = 232$

6. $47 \times 9 = (40 + 7) \times 9 = 40 \times 9 + 7 \times 9 = 360 + 63 = 423$

In the Proper Order . . . . .page 44

1. $17 + 3 \times (18 - 7) = 17 + 3 \times 11 = 17 + 33 = 50$

2. $(11 + 14) \div 5 + 7 = 25 \div 5 + 7 = 5 + 7 = 12$

3. $(12 - 7) \times (33 - 25) = 5 \times 8 = 40$

4. $8 + 56 \div 7 - 9 = 8 + 8 - 9 = 16 - 9 = 7$

5. $(7 + 8 - 4) \times 5 - 10 = (15 - 4) \times 5 - 10 = 11 \times 5 - 10 = 55 - 10 = 45$

6. $19 + 12 \div 3 - 6 \times 3 = 19 + 4 - 18 = 23 - 18 = 5$

Digit Dilemma . . . . .page 45

1. 364

2. 757 or 737

3. 4,515

4. 803

0-7424-2884-2 *Using the Standards—Algebra*

Answer Key

Number Clues . . . . .page 46
   1. 3,256
   2. 7,062
   3. 47,813
   4. 52,446

Mystery Numbers . . . . .page 47
   1. 5
   2. 15
   3. 9
   4. 12
   5. 11

Missing Numbers . . . . .page 48
   1. $y = 11$ **5.** $s = 7$ **9.** $m = 26$
   2. $c = 6$ **6.** $g = 40$ **10.** $z = 13$
   3. $k = 20$ **7.** $d = 33$ **11.** $v = 27$
   4. $a = 2$ **8.** $h = 32$ **12.** $w = 28$

Solve It! . . . . .page 49
   1. ♡ $= 14$
   2. $L = 84$
   3. ♣ $= 12$
   4. $T = 55$
   5. ☾ $= 38$
   6. $P = 21$

Valuable Variables . . . . .page 50
   1. ☆ $= 238$
   2. $M = 54$
   3. △ $= 22$
   4. $P = 2,265$
   5. ⬡ $= 7,868$
   6. $R = 321$
   7. ➡ $= 1,584$
   8. $V = 23$

Solution Pairs . . . . .page 51
   1. a. $m = 3, p = 12$ **3. a.** $r = 1, s = 12$
      b. $m = 2, p = 8$ **b.** $r = 9, s = 4$
      c. $m = 9, p = 36$ **c.** $r = 4, s = 9$
   2. a. $h = 15, j = 3$ **4. a.** $d = 4, f = 6$
      b. $h = 25, j = 13$ **b.** $d = 3, f = 8$
      c. $h = 20, j = 8$ **c.** $d = 2, f = 12$

A Sporting Chance . . . . .page 52
   1. $D = 26; J = 32; T = 26; A = 16$
   2. $F = 14; B = 12; H = 6$
   3. $F = 3; B = 5; H = 8$
   4. $F = 15; B = 1; H = 10$
   5. $F = 7; B = 10; H = 9$

A Baker's Dozen . . . . .page 53
   1. $C = 15; S = 7; P = 7; O = 7$
   2. $C = 20; S = 18; P = 10; O = 12$
   3. $C = 15; S = 25; P = 50; O = 10$
   4. $C = 3; S = 12; P = 13; O = 20$

Nature Walk . . . . .page 54
   1. $B = 12; S = 4; D = 5$
   2. $B = 14; S = 8; R = 2; C = 6$
   3. $B = 3; S = 2; D = 4; R = 3; N = 6$
   4. $B = 20; S = 1; C = 5; R = 4; D = 8; N = 2$

Symbol Sense .page 55
   1. △ $= 5$, ☐ $= 6$ (or vice versa)
   2. ⬡ $= 12$, ☐ $= 2$
   3. 🌹 $= 8$, 🦀 $= 7$ (or vice versa)
   4. ➡ $= 25$, ☆ $= 4$
   5. ☾ $= 5$, ◯ $= 20$
   6. ◇ $= 4$, △ $= 9$

Alphabet Soup .page 56
   1. $W = 2, Y = 6$
   2. $B = 20, C = 4$
   3. $K = 5, L = 10$
   4. $M = 40, N = 18$
   5. $D = 7, F = 18$
   6. $P = 4, Q = 20$
   7. $T = 3, V = 5$
   8. $H = 16, J = 25$

Triple Tease . . . . .page 57
   1. △ $= 5$; ☐ $= 15$; ⬡ $= 8$
   2. ◯ $= 9$; ◇ $= 6$; ☆ $= 5$
   3. ⬠ $= 2$; ◗ $= 9$; ☐ $= 8$
   4. ⬯ $= 4$; △ $= 1$; ☾ $= 12$

Exceptional Equations . . . . pages 58–59
   1. a. $J = H + 4$ **3. a.** $15 \times N = T$
      b. $H = 12, J = 16$ **b.** $N = 6, T = 90$
      c. $H = 8, J = 12$ **c.** $N = 8, T = 120$
   2. a. $Y = T - 16$ **4. a.** $B \times 32 = P$
      b. $Y = 39, T = 55$ **b.** $B = 4, P = 128$
      c. $Y = 60, T = 76$ **c.** $B = 6, P = 192$

That's a Puzzler . . . . .page 60
   1. $N = $ # of pieces already put together
   2. $114 + N = 500$
   3. $N = 386$
   4. Hannah has put together 386 pieces of the puzzle.

    0-7424-2884-2 *Using the Standards—Algebra*

Answer Key

Picture Perfect . . . . page 61

1. R = # of rolls of film
2. # rolls of film x # of pictures on each roll = total # of pictures
3. $R \times 24 = 360$
4. $R = 15$
5. The memory card replaces 15 rolls of film.

A Sweet Treat . . . . page 62

1. B = # of candy bars the class ate
2. total # of candy bars − # of candy bars the class ate = # of candy bars left
3. $250 − B = 75$
4. $B = 175$
5. The class ate 175 candy bars.

Taking a Trip . . . . page 63

1. C = # of chaperones
2. # of students ÷ # of students per chaperone = # of chaperones
3. $75 ÷ 5 = C$
4. $C = 15$
5. They will need 15 chaperones on the trip.

Finding Unknowns . . . . pages 64–65

1. **a.** t = Number of tables
   b. $t \times 6 = 108$
   c. $t = 108 / 6$
   $t = 18$
   18 Tables are needed.
2. **a.** m = number of miles left to ride
   b. $438 + m = 1000$
   c. $m = 1000 − 438$
   $m = 562$
   Bai can ride 562 more miles before his bike needs a tune up.
3. **a.** c = number of coins per page
   b. $c \times 53 = 1060$
   c. $c = 1060 / 53$
   $c = 20$
   Each page holds 20 coins.
4. **a.** b = number of bulbs planted.
   b. $28 + b = 72$
   c. $b = 72 − 28$
   $b = 44$
   Kevin has planted 44 bulbs so far.

Perplexing Problems . . . . pages 66–67

1. **a.** $C + R = 18$
   b. $C = C + 8$
   c. $C = 13 \ C = 5$
2. **a.** $H + V = 20$
   b. $H = V + 8$
   c. $H = 14, V = 6$
3. **a.** $A = 18 / 3$
   b. $A + S = 10$
   c. $A = 6, S = 4, T = 8$
4. **a.** $F + S = 54$
   b. $F = 4 \times 6$
   c. $F = 24, S = 30$

How Far? . . . . page 68

1. $D = 60 \times 5$
   $D = 300$ miles
2. $D = 12 \times 2$
   $D = 24$ miles
3. $D = 570 \times 4$
   $D = 2280$ miles
4. $D = 40 \times 3$
   $D = 120$ miles

How Fast? . . . . page 69

1. $8 = R \times 4$
   $R = 8 / 4$
   $R = 2$ km/h
2. $5 = R \times 1.25$
   $R = 5 / 1.25$
   $R = 4$ m/h
3. $420 = R \times 7$
   $R = 420 / 7$
   $R = 60$ m/h
4. $36 = R \times 3$
   $R = 36 / 3$
   $R = 12$ m/h

How Long? . . . . page 70

1. $1500 = 500 \times T$
   $T = 1500 / 500$
   $T = 3$ hours
2. $60 = 15 \times T$
   $T = 60 / 15$
   $T = 4$ hours
3. $5 = 3 \times T$
   $T = 5 / 3$
   $T = 1.6$ hours ($1\frac{2}{3}$ hours)
4. $195 = 65 \times T$
   $T = 195 / 65$
   $T = 3$ hours

Check Your Skills . . . . pages 72–73

1. **a.** $7 + (9 + 12)$; associative OR $12 + (7 + 9)$; commutative
   b. $6 \times 15 + 6 \times 32$; distributive
   c. 26×3; commutative
2. 6,102
3. **a.** ☘ = 491
   b. ☾ = 5
   c. ☆ = 16
   d. ◇ = 163
4. $M = 20; C = 10; V = 15$
5. **a.** $B = 3, D = 15$ (or vice versa)
   b. $R = 4, T = 12$

0-7424-2884-2 *Using the Standards—Algebra*

Answer Key

6. a. $A = D - 23$
   b. $D = 60$, $A = 37$
   c. $D = 53$, $A = 30$
7. a. $280 = R \times 4$ OR $R = 280 \div 4$
   b. $R = 70$ miles/hour

Weighty Matters . . . . pages 74–75

Teacher's Note: All answers below refer to U.S. currency.

1. quarter
2. $2P = Q$
3. a. 4 pennies; $2P \times 2 = Q \times 2$; $4P = 2Q$
   b. 4 quarters; $2P \times 4 = Q \times 4$; $8P = 4Q$
   c. 12 pennies; $2P \times 6 = Q \times 6$; $12P = 6Q$
4. yes
5. penny
6. $5D = 4P$
7. a. 8 pennies; $5D \times 2 = 4P \times 2$; $10D = 8P$
   b. 15 dimes; $5D \times 3 = 4P \times 3$; $15D = 12P$
   c. 16 pennies; $5D \times 4 = 4P \times 4$; $20D = 16P$
8. yes
9. $5D = 2Q$; $5D = 4P$; $4P = 2Q$; $5D = 4P = 2Q$
10. yes

Container Calculations . . . . pages 76–77

Teacher's Note: An 18 oz. empty cylindrical oatmeal container and a box that held 20 gallon-size reclosable storage bags were used for this experiment. The answers below reflect these containers. Your results may differ depending on the containers chosen.

1. Answers may vary.
2. The cylinder.
3. Answers may vary.
4. $A = s^2$
5. $V = H \times s^2$
6. $V = h \times 3.14 \times r^2$
7. prism: $s = 2.5$ in., $H = 11.5$ in.; cylinder: $r = 2$ in., $h = 7$ in.
8. prism: $V = 2.5 \times 2.5 \times 11.5 = 71.875$ in.^{3}
   cylinder: $V = 3.14 \times 2^2 \times 7 = 87.92$ in.^{3}

Recreational Rectangles . . . . pages 78–79

1. Make sure students double-check the noodle lengths.
2. a. 22 in.
   b. Cut the remaining piece in half.
   c. $L = 11$ in.

3.

width	1	2	3	4	5	6	7	8	9
length	11	10	9	8	7	6	5	4	3

4. There are 6 different rectangles. A 7 by 5 rectangle is the same size as a 5 by 7 rectangle.
5. Answers may vary.

Perimeter Puzzle . . . . pages 80–81

1. a. Check lengths of spaghetti noodles.
   b. 12 cm
   c. Cut the remaining piece in half.
   d. $L = 6$ cm

2.

W	5	5	5	5
P	22	20	18	16
L	6	5	4	3

3. Possible Answer: Multiply the width of 5 by 2 because there are 2 sides. This gives you 10 cm. Subtract this from the perimeter. That will give you the amount of fencing left for the top and bottom. Divide this by 2 so the top and bottom will be the same length.
4. $L = (P - 10) \div 2$ OR $L = P \div 2 - 5$

5.

W	5	6	7	8
P	20	26	22	26
L	5	7	4	5

6. Possible Answer: Multiply the width by 2 because there are 2 sides. Subtract this from the perimeter. That will give you the amount of fencing left for the top and bottom. Divide this by 2 so the top and bottom will be the same length.

To the Max . . . . pages 82–83

1. Make sure students double-check the noodle lengths.

2.

width	1	2	3	4	5	6	7	8	9
length	9	8	7	6	5	4	3	2	1

3. Answers may vary.
4. Answers may vary.

5.

width	1	2	3	4	5	6	7	8	9
length	9	8	7	6	5	4	3	2	1
area	9	16	21	24	25	24	21	16	9

6. 5 by 5

7.

width	1	2	3	4	5	6	7	8	9	10
length	15	14	13	12	11	10	9	8	7	6
area	15	28	39	48	55	60	63	64	63	60

8.

width	1	2	3	4	5	6	7	8	9	10
length	13	12	11	10	9	8	7	6	5	4
area	13	24	33	40	45	48	49	48	45	40

Check Your Skills . . . . page 85

1. a. $Q = P \times 2$
   b. 22 pennies
   c. 15 quarters
2. a. Check models
   b. 6 sq. cm
   c. 7
   d. $7 \times 6 = 42$ cu. cm
   e. $V = L \times W \times H$
3. a. $L = 8 - W$
   b. 4 cm by 4 cm

0-7424-2884-2 *Using the Standards—Algebra*

Answer Key

Stretched to the Limit . . . . .pages 86–87

  1. Predictions may vary. Students will probably guess that the rubber band will stretch longer when more weight is added. Get them to be more specific (i.e. constant rate or not constant, how much will it stretch for each penny added, etc.).

2–4. Answers will vary depending on experimental results.

  5. As the weight increases by 1 penny, the length increases by about x centimeters (amount of increase will vary).

  6. Predictions will vary.

Up and Down . . . . .pages 88–89

  1. The height of the ball started a couple of feet above the ground. Then it increased until it hit its highest point. Then it decreased, past the point it started until it hit the ground.

  2. The ball slowed down on its way up, until it stopped at its highest point. Then the ball's speed increased due to gravity as it fell back down to the ground.

  3. Graph D shows the relationship.

4–6. Answers will vary depending on experimental results.

  7. The graphs should have the same shape as graph D from problem 3. The axes should have a scale that fits the measurements found in problems 4–6. The graph should match the starting height, maximum height, and time measurements taken in the experiment.

FAN-tastic! . . . . .pages 90–91

  1.

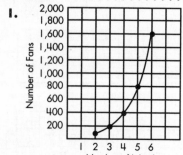

  2. The graph increases in a curved pattern.

  3. The number of fans doubles each month.

  4. 1,600 x 2 = 3,200 fans

  5. 9 months; Students should extend the table, doubling the number of fans each month.

  6. 204,800 fans

Making Money .pages 92–93

  1. $10; $15

  2.

# of hours	1	2	3	4	5	6
amt. earned	5	10	15	20	25	30

  3.

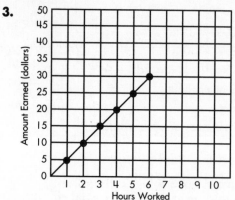

  4. Each time the number of hours increases by 1, the amount of money she earns increases by $5.

  5. $27.50; students may use the table or graph or perform a calculation.

  6. 9 hours; students may extend the table or graph or perform a calculation.

  7. $A = 5 \times H$

  8. $200; $A = 5 \times 40 = \$200$

Ferris Wheel . . . . .pages 94–95

  1. The boys were at the top of the Ferris Wheel. Look at 0 seconds on the graph. The graph is at 70 ft. which is the highest point on the graph. So, the boys had to be at the top.

  2. The bottom of the Ferris Wheel is 10 ft. above the ground. The lowest points on the graph are at 10 ft.

  3. The center of the Ferris Wheel is 40 feet off the ground. That's halfway between the highest point, 70 ft., and the lowest point, 10 ft.

  4. The Ferris Wheel takes 2 minutes (120 seconds) to make one revolution. At 0 seconds the graph shows the boys were at 70 ft. The next time the graph shows they are at that height is at 120 seconds.

  5. The boys were at the bottom of the Ferris Wheel when the ride ended. They were at the lowest point of the graph (10 ft.) at 180 seconds, which is 3 minutes.

  6. No. The Ferris wheel travels around in a circle.

  7. The ride was 180 seconds. So halfway would be at 90 seconds. The graph shows that the boys were 40 ft. above the ground at that time.

  8. The boys made $1\frac{1}{2}$ revolutions. They started at 70 ft. (the top), returned to 70 ft. (the top) at 120 seconds (2 minutes) and then ended at the bottom of the Ferris Wheel.

Cube Curiosity .pages 96–97

  1.

stage	0	1	2	3	4	5	6
volume	1	2	5	7	9	11	13

0-7424-2884-2 *Using the Standards—Algebra*

Answer Key

2. As the stage increases by 1, the volume increases by 2 cubes. The volume changes at a constant rate. The table shows the numbers for volume going up by 2 each time.

3. 21 cubes; Students may extend the table and use the pattern to find the answer.

4.

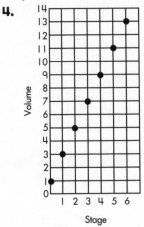

5. $V = 1 + 2 \times S$

Teacher's Note: Students may have difficulties getting this equation. Refer them back to the physical models and ask leading questions. They started with one cube and added 2 cubes for each stage. So, at stage 7 they would have added 2 x 7, or 14, cubes to the first cube, for a total of 15 cubes.

6.

stage	0	1	2	3	4	5	6
volume	6	14	22	30	38	46	54

7. As the stage increases by 1, the surface area increases by 8 square units. This is a constant rate of change. The table shows the surface area values going up by 8 each time.

8. 86 square units; Students may extend the table and use the pattern to find the answer.

9.

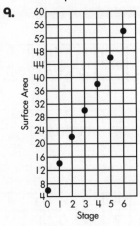

10. $A = 6 + 8 \times S$

Teacher's Note: Students may have difficulties getting this equation. Refer them back to the physical models and ask leading questions. They started with 6 square units of surface area and added 8 square units for each stage. So, at stage 7 they would have added 8 x 7, or 56, square units to the first 6 square units, for a total of 62 square units.

Building Pyramids . . . . **pages 98–99**

1.

stage	0	1	2	3	4	5	6
volume	1	4	9	16	25	36	49

2. The volume increases. No, it doesn't change at a constant rate. First it goes up by 3, then by 5, and then by 7.

3. The volume increases in a pattern by adding consecutive odd integers: + 3, + 5, + 7, + 9, + 11, + 13...

4. 81 cubes; Students should extend the table to eight stages.

5.

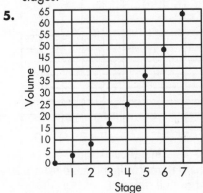

Dollars and Sense . . . . **pages 100–101**

1. Answers may vary.

2.

# of days	1	2	3	4	5	6	7	8	9	10	11	12	13	14	15
total $ earned	2	4	6	8	10	12	14	16	18	20	22	24	26	28	30

3. Constant rate. The total earned increases by $2 each day.

4.

# of days	1	2	3	4	5	6	7	8
$ amt. earned	0.01	0.02	0.04	0.08	0.16	0.32	0.64	1.28
total $ earned	0.01	0.03	0.07	0.15	0.31	0.63	1.27	2.55

# of days	9	10	11	12	13	14	15	16
$ amt. earned	2.56	5.12	10.24	20.48	40.96	81.92	163.84	
total $ earned	5.11	10.23	20.47	40.95	81.91	163.83	327.67	

5. Varying rate. The total increases by a different amount each time.

6. The first plan would be better. Jeremy would make $20 compared to $10.23.

7. The second plan would be better. Jeremy would make $327.67, which is a lot more than $30.

119

Answer Key

8. Jeremy should accept his mother's plan if he works less than 12 days.

9. Jeremy would do better with his own plan if he works 12 days or more.

Speeding Spectacular . . . . .page 102

1. $S = 400 ÷ T$

2.
Time	4	5	6	7	8	9	10
Speed	100	80	67	57	50	44	40

3. As the time of the trip increases, the average speed decreases.

4.
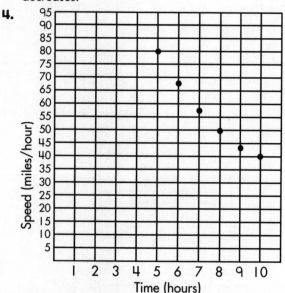

5. Varying rate. The differences in the table from one value to the next are all different ($-13, -10, -7, -6, -4$). The graph has a curve, not a straight line.

Go Gravity! . . . . .page 103

1. As the time increases, the height of the penny decreases.

2. Varying Rate. The graph is curved, so the interval between each second is different every time.

3. Just over $4\frac{1}{2}$ seconds. Look at the where the graph hits the horizontal axis, which is a height of 0. This is when the penny hit the ground.

4. 80 meters. Find 2 seconds on the graph. Follow the grid line up until it hits the graph. Look over to see the height, which is 80 meters.

Give It Some Bounce . . . . .pages 104–105
Answers will vary.

Check Your Skills . . . . .pages 107–108

1. a. Constant rate. The difference in the table from one value to the next are all the same (+ 2).

   b. $L = 24 + 2 \times W$

   c. 48 inches

2. a. $9, $15

   b. 9 hours

   c. $M = $3 \times H$

3. a.
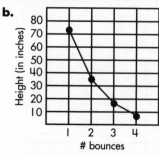

# bounces	1	2	3	4
height (in inches)	72	36	18	9

b.

c. Varying rate. The difference between each pair of values is not the same.

4. Constant rate of change: b, d
   Varying rate of change: a, c

Posttest . . . . .pages 109–110

1. a. 29, 36, 44; (+ 1, + 2, + 3, + 4...); varying rate

   b. 42, 47, 52; add 5 each time; constant rate

   c. 102, 165, 267; add the previous two numbers to get the next number; varying rate

2. OUT = IN + 12

IN	10	6	15	22	18	44
OUT	22	18	27	34	30	56

3. a. commutative

   b. distributive

   c. associative

4. a. 🌷 = 5, 🦀 = 10

   b. ♡ = 20, ◇ = 2

5. a. $A = S + 9$

   b. $A = 52, S = 43$

   c. $A = 42, S = 34$

6. a.
length	1	2	3	4	5	6	7	8	9	10	11	12	13
width	25	24	23	22	21	20	19	18	17	16	15	14	13

   b. 13 by 13

7. a.
Stage	0	1	2	3	4	5
Area	4	8	12	16	20	24

   b $A = 4 + 4 \times S$

   c. constant rate

8. a.
Hours	1	2	3	4	5	6	7	8
Amt. in $	2	4	6	8	10	12	14	16

   b. $A = 2 \times H$

   c. $30; $A = 2 \times 15$

0-7424-2884-2 *Using the Standards—Algebra*

repeating pattern	**growing pattern**
decreasing pattern	**rules**
constant rate	**varying rate**

0-7424-2884-2 *Using the Standards—Algebra*

a series of numbers that gets larger using a rule

5, 9, 13, 17, 21

Rule: + 4

---

a series of numbers, letters, shapes, or other objects that repeat in a certain order

3   3   4   4

---

describes the process used to create a pattern or tells how to change numbers in a function machine

− 10 or OUT = IN x 3

---

a series of numbers that gets smaller using a rule

35, 33, 32, 30, 28

Rule: − 2

---

when a variable changes by different amounts each time

Example:

time	distance
1	10
2	14
3	19
4	26
5	35

---

when a variable changes by the same amount each time

Example:

time	distance
1	10
2	20
3	30
4	40

0-7424-2884-2 *Using the Standards—Algebra*

function machine	commutative property
associative property	distributive property
order of operations	variable

0-7424-2884-2 *Using the Standards—Algebra*

changing the order of the numbers does not change the answer

$7 \times 4 = 4 \times 7$ $5 + 9 = 9 + 5$
$28 = 28$ $14 = 14$

uses a rule to change IN numbers to OUT numbers

IN	55	38	72	61	80
OUT	26	9	43	32	51

Rule: OUT = IN − 29

a way to rewrite multiplication over addition without changing the answer

$3 \times (5 + 7) = 3 \times 5 + 3 \times 7$
$3 \times 12 = 15 + 21$
$36 = 36$

changing the grouping of the numbers does not change the answer

$(14 + 12) + 8 = 14 + (12 + 8)$
$26 + 8 = 14 + 20$
$34 = 34$

a letter or symbol that stands for an unknown number

$3 \times \textcircled{T} = 18$

tells in which sequence operations should be performed to get the right answer

Parentheses, Exponents, Multiplication, Division, Addition, Subtraction

0-7424-2884-2 *Using the Standards—Algebra*

distance equation

model

area of a rectangle

equivalent

rate

coordinate graph

0-7424-2884-2 *Using the Standards—Algebra*

using objects, sketches, or mathematical equations to represent a situation

shows the relationship between distance traveled, average speed, and time

D = R x T

has the same value, but is written differently

5 + *T* = 10 means the same as *T* = 10 − 5

A = L x W

a graph using points to show the relationship between two variables

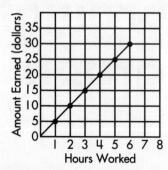

a comparison of two different kinds of units

miles per hour
dollars per hour
hours per week

126

0-7424-2884-2 *Using the Standards—Algebra*

area of a circle	volume of a cylinder
volume of a rectangular prism	**sum**
product	**difference**

0-7424-2884-2 *Using the Standards—Algebra*

$$V = (3.14 \times r^2) \times H$$

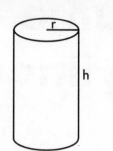

$$A = 3.14 \times r^2$$

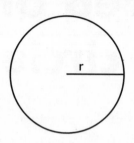

the answer to an addition problem

$82 + 35 = \boxed{117}$

$$V = L \times W \times H$$

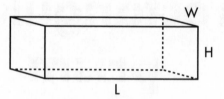

the answer to a subtraction problem

$117 - 82 = \boxed{35}$

the answer to a multiplication problem

$3 \times 14 = \boxed{42}$

0-7424-2884-2 *Using the Standards—Algebra*